A PASSION
FOR DEMOCRACY

~

Benjamin Constant

by Tzvetan Todorov

By the same author, in English translation:

Facing the Extreme (Holt, 1996)

A French Tragedy (University Press of New England, 1996)

The Morals of History (University of Minnesota Press, 1995)

On Human Diversity (Harvard University Press, 1993)

Genres in Discourse (Cambridge University Press, 1990)

Literature and Its Theorists (Cornell University Press, 1987)

The Conquest of America (University of Oklahoma Press, 1999; HarperCollins, 1984)

Theories of the Symbol (Cornell University Press, 1982)

Symbolism and Interpretation (Cornell University Press, 1982)

Mikhail Bakhtin, The Dialogical Principle (University of Minnesota Press, 1981)

Introduction to Poetics (University of Michigan Press, 1981)

Encyclopedic Dictionary of the Sciences of Language (with O. Ducrot, Johns Hopkins University Press, 1979)

The Poetics of Prose (Cornell University Press, 1977)

The Fantastic (Cornell University Press, 1975)

A Passion for Democracy —

BENJAMIN CONSTANT

by

TZVETAN TODOROV

Translated
by Alice Seberry

Algora Publishing

Originally published as *Benjamin Constant, La Passion démocratique,*
© Éditions Hachette Littératures, 1997.

Library of Congress Cataloging-in-Publication Data 99-33966
Todorov, Tzvetan, 1939-
    [Benjamin Constant. English]
    A Passion for Democracy / Tzvetan Todorov; translated from
French by Alice Seberry.
        p.   cm.
Includes bibliographical references.
ISBN 1-892941-01-5 (alk. paper)
1. Constant, Benjamin, 1767-1830—Contributions in political sci-
ence. 2. Democracy.   I. Title.
JC229.C8T6313 1999
320.5′ 12′ 092—dc21

The paper used in this publication meets the minimum requirements of the American National Standard for Information Sciences—Permanence of Paper for Printed Library Materials, ANSI
Z39.48-1992.

New York
www.algora.com

References given within parentheses refer to publications listed at the end of the book. The last number designates the page of the quoted text; the number immediately prior designates the internal subdivision of the cited text (the part, section, or chapter number).

For Paul Bénichou

Table of Contents

Table of Contents

The Elusive Constant

We might begin by expressing our astonishment—how is it that Benjamin Constant is not considered among the most prestigious authors in the history of French literature? Isn't he the first great thinker of liberal democracy, the author of a vast and profound meditation on religion, a lucid and ironic autobiographer? Isn't his diary one of the most amazing explorations of the vagaries of the human soul ever undertaken? Isn't his one novel, *Adolphe,* an undisputed masterpiece? Wasn't he recognized and admired by some of his greatest contemporaries — Goethe, Pushkin, Stendhal and Hugo? Yet, at the end of the 20th century, Constant's name is nearly forgotten, or is placed at best with second-rate writers. Critics often treat him with a bit of condescension. "Poor Benjamin!," they exclaim, before moving on to more serious subjects. Certainly, he is a "classic," but his most important work on religion, for example, has still never been reprinted.

This relative oblivion surely has several explanations. One is that liberal thought in France has long been overshadowed by Marxist historiography, which is especially influential in this field. Another is the fact that Constant's political thought corresponds so closely to our current democracies; it seems so natural to us that we have trouble seeing it. Yet another explanation derives from the very richness of his work, which is difficult to classify. Is Constant a writer, or a philosopher? A scholar, a historian, or a sociologist? A fourth explanation might be found in the history of his writings. Actively involved in the political life of his time, Constant did not give all the necessary attention to publishing his works. His treatise on religion had not been entirely printed at the time of his death, his personal writings were not published in their final form until the middle of the 20th century, and his fundamental political texts only saw the light of day in 1980 and 1991.

But there are also reasons inherent to his message that explain why it has been difficult to recognize the true quality of his work. Among liberals themselves Constant is, in certain respects, an exception. He is probably the first French writer with a resolutely anti-

heroic attitude, who treats writing itself in a desacralized manner, a fact that has prevented us from seeing his greatness. For this very reason, however, the contemporary reader feels on equal terms with the author in Constant's work, especially in his personal writings. Not only does Constant not praise the heroic ideal nor cast himself in the heroic role, he is not even inclined, like Rousseau, to take pride in his faults. No one before him had admitted his flaws with such simplicity. He doesn't make a show of them, he simply notes them — and occasionally laughs at them. He does not display the slightest urge to total mastery or proud domination in this sincere and open work; far from presenting himself as a self-sufficient being, Constant recognizes his vulnerability and dependence on others. This is probably why a few narrow-minded spirits have long pursued him with their calumnies and violent hostility. Taking advantage of his refusal to present himself as a hero, as a superman dominating the human herd (what a contrast in this respect between Constant and his near-contemporaries such as Chateaubriand and Tocqueville!), they have seized upon his "weaknesses" and reproach him with them, as if they could not forgive him for having shaken the very notion of idolatry.

Constant appears to us today as the first fully "modern" French author, through his sensibility but also through his thought. The Revolution began when he was twenty-two years old; consequently he was present at the birth of the contemporary world. But sometimes he seems even closer to us; he is detached not only from the *Ancien Regime*, but also from the opposing movements of thought and action that the 19th and 20th centuries would bring to bear: blind materialism, nihilism and totalitarianism. In every instance, his thought embraces both sides of the conflict and goes beyond them to establish what could be called modern humanism, equidistant from traditional spiritualism and "scientific" materialism. This choice creates in him a happy combination of lucidity and compassion (a pitiless lucidity about himself and a deeply-felt compassion for others). Constant is a psychologist capable of revealing the secret selfish motivations of apparently virtuous acts; but his keen awareness of human limitations prevents this clairvoyance from becoming misanthropy. He renounces neither the true nor the good, he is a political man who is simultaneously committed and despairing: committed because he would like to make the world better, despairing because he will never cease to be lucid. How can he reconcile love of truth and love of the good? Constant is torn between aspiration to the infinite and awareness of our finitude, but he sees in this division the very truth of modern man.

It is also very refreshing that Constant is as far removed from the politician who turns to writing to give himself an intellectual aura as he is from the theorist who is more interested in the rigor and beauty of his constructs than in their translation into everyday application. Constant never lets himself be dazzled by words; he wants to know to what facts they correspond (often fine words conceal shameful acts). While skilled in manipulating abstractions, he knows how to convert them into concrete reality. It is precisely this quality that enables him to maintain the continuity between reflection and activism. With him, theory and practice sustain each other. The political man meditates on his experiences by writing treatises, whose ideas he subsequently transforms for the benefit of his new political activities; the passionate man distills bitter lessons from his life in his personal and literary writings, which in turn transform his emotional life.

Constant's thought suffers from its very qualities: its closeness to us makes it almost invisible. In many respects, it corresponds to the implicit foundation of our own acts, we who as autonomous subjects of modern nations do not necessarily have access to the Divine, but who do not therefore abandon all belief in transcendence, and who do not believe that the world is exclusively governed by self-interest or the will to power. We must therefore make an effort to rescue this thought from its transparency, and read it.

A Multifaceted Work

Biography

We should start with a quick overview of a personality in which political and sentimental commitments were closely intermingled, and whose body of work is particularly difficult to grasp in its diversity. (For more biographical details, refer to the chronology which appears at the end of this book.)

Benjamin Constant was born in 1767 in Lausanne, into a Huguenot family whose ancestors had left France in the 17th century. His mother, twenty-five years old, died of complications fifteen days after this first childbirth. The father, a career soldier, lived in Holland. The paternal and maternal families disputed custody of the child, and initially the maternal side won. However, from 1772 onward, the father regained custody and left the child with various tutors, frequently replaced. Constant was therefore often required to change his place of residence as well. In 1783, he enrolled at the University of Edinburgh, where he stayed for almost two years. He then returned to the continent, staying in Switzerland and in Paris, where he became acquainted with Mme. de Charrière, a woman of letters and a caustic spirit, 27 years his elder, who would influence him considerably. In 1788, he was installed as chamberlain at the court of the Duke of Brunswick; there he met Minna von Cramm, who became his wife the following year. He began work on various writings related to history, religion and politics. In 1793, he separated from his wife and moved back to Switzerland where, in 1794, he met Germaine de Staël, née Necker, wife of the Swedish ambassador in Paris but living apart from him, and who had already published several works of note.

Thus ends the first period of Constant's life, marked by great emotional chaos and by equally confused studies (which, nonetheless, reveal the youth's early intellectual maturity), and especially by a sharp curiosity about the political and literary world. Meeting Mme. de Staël profoundly upset this life and inaugurated a second period, from 1794 to 1802, during which Constant alternated between stays in Switzerland and France, taking his first steps in the public life of France, writing several texts on political theory, and deepening his study of religion. He quickly took up with Mme. de Staël, but began living with her only a year and a half later. A daughter, Albertine, would be born to them in 1797. Constant felt a great intellectual admiration for Mme. de Staël and, during these years, their thoughts influenced each other mutually; their emotional intimacy, on the other hand, faded quickly.

In 1802, Constant was ejected from the Tribunat. More and more, Napoleon was concentrating power in his own hands. Mme. de Staël was banished from France; Constant followed her, even while thinking of breaking off the relationship — possibly by marrying someone else. He accompanied her to Germany in 1803-1804, where he became acquainted with Goethe, Schiller, Wieland and the Schlegel brothers. He married Charlotte von Hardenberg, a German whom he had known at Brunswick, in 1808, but decided to leave Mme. de Staël once and for all only in 1811. After that date he settled with Charlotte in Germany, where he stayed until 1814, when the defeat of Napoleon enabled him to return to Paris. During this period, 1802-1814, Constant lived as an exile and he was often quite unhappy. This was the most fertile period of his life in terms of literature and philosophy; all his important works were begun then. He wrote the first version of his great work on religion, completed both parts of a treatise on political theory, wrote a short novel (which later became *Adolphe*), produced an astonishing *Journal Intime* [Diary] and left unfinished two autobiographical accounts, *Ma Vie* (called by its first editors *Le Cahier rouge*) and *Cécile*.

Having returned to Paris in 1814, Constant sought to rejoin French political life. He published *De l'esprit de conquête et de l'usurpation*, on the principles of politics. This was actually an assemblage of pieces from an earlier work that remained unpublished (Constant would repeat this process several times thereafter). In September, he fell passionately in love with Juliette Récamier, without succeeding to engender the least reciprocity. Upon the Napoleon's return during the Hundred Days, he agreed to collaborate with the Emperor. After Napoleon's abdication, he rallied to the monarchy. He left Paris in October 1815, fleeing both his political enemies and his unhappy love affair with Mme. Récamier. He went back to Charlotte and settled with her in London, where he finished and published *Adolphe*, which met a certain success. He returned then to Paris, this time for good, at the end of 1816.

During the last period of his life (1817-1830), Constant led an easier existence in terms of sentiment; politically, he became one of the leaders of the liberal opposition, and was elected to the Assembly several times. In his writings and his speeches, he participated in all the political battles of his era. He also rewrote his work on religion, and published the first volume in 1824. The last two volumes (IV-V) would appear in 1831, after his death. He also combined several other sets of writings, political and literary. The revolution of July 1830 was perceived as a victory by the liberals, who supported the establishment of Louis Philippe.

Constant, already quite ill, was celebrated and honored. He died in December of the same year; a large crowd turned out for his funeral.

Inventory

It is hard to grasp Constant's writings as a whole. His work branches out in many directions, which are far from easy to articulate. This diversity strongly influenced his perception among readers; and, during Constant's lifetime, most of his work remained unpublished. For his contemporaries, he was above all a man and a writer of politics. His literary work was noticed, but did not have much impact. Nor did the work on religion draw much response. For Constant himself, things were altogether different. We now know that he had finished his work on political philosophy in 1806 and that he was satisfied, thereafter, to publish excerpts and paraphrases from it, sometimes adapted to the circumstances of the moment. It was the work on religion that was dearest to his heart, and to which he devoted literally his entire life, that is — with interruptions — from 1785 to 1830! On the other hand, to the 20th century reader, Constant is mostly known as the author of *Adolphe*, that "masterpiece of the psychological novel," as well as a few autobiographical and personal writings that would be published in their entirety only in the middle of the 20th century.

Today, nearly all of Constant's work has been printed and, even if some titles are not easy to find, it has become possible to form a comprehensive picture and to attempt a general interpretation of this abundant work. First, let us draw up an inventory list that identifies the major groupings.

1. At the top of the list, by virtue of their volume, his political writings. How they were perceived is much affected by the circumstances that prevailed when they were published, which one can summarize in three stages.

a) At the very beginning of the 19th century Constant wrote a large treatise on political theory, which he ended up dividing into two separate texts. "This," he later wrote while speaking of his work, "originally consisted of two parts, the constitutional institutions and the rights of individuals, in other words the means of guaranteeing freedom and the principles of freedom." (*Principes*, 1806, "Additions," 512). These two works, the first dedicated to the Republican constitution (*Constitution républicaine*, completed in about 1802), the second entitled *Principes de politique* (finished in 1806), were not published during Constant's lifetime — under Napoleon, because it would have been inconceivable; later, because Constant had already published excerpts separately. These works would appear in their entirety only in 1980, for the second part, and in 1991 for the first.

b) From 1814 until his death in 1830, Constant would publish many works, pamphlets, articles and speeches, whose contents are drawn mainly from these two unpublished volumes. The most significant are *De l'esprit de conquête et de l'usurpation* (1814), the new *Principes de politique* (1815), *De la liberté des Anciens comparée à celle des Modernes* (1819) and *Commentaire sur les ouvrages de Filangieri* (1822-1824).

c) Lastly, Constant also had in mind, while he was alive, to impose some order on this prolific output, and he collated the earlier partial publications as well as some of the unpublished works in several collective volumes: *Cours de politique consitutionnelle* in four volumes (1818-1819), *Mélanges de littérature et de politique* (1829) and, in a somewhat different vein, *Discours à la Chambre des députés,* in two volumes (1827-1828). The same page would often be rewritten three or four times: deepening the thought, adapting it to the needs of the moment, taking into account the censor's requirements. Constant's posthumous editors continued to rearrange these collections whose purpose, to some extent, is to retrieve the unity of the unpublished manuscripts.

In addition to this ensemble, we must count among the political writings his many occasional texts, *Mémoires sur les Cent-Jours,* as well as his responses to new doctrines, in particular to Saint-Simonism (i.e. socialism).

2. We should also mention, early on, the work on religion. Constant devoted himself to this throughout

his life. It was published beginning in 1824, five volumes in all, under the title *De la religion, considerée dans sa source, ses formes et ses développements.* Add to that various articles published during his lifetime, as well as many drafts and preliminary versions of the final works, published after his death, including two volumes of *Polythéisme romain,* following the main work but also re-using fragments which already appeared in *Religion.* These works have never been republished.

3. A third group, far fewer in number but of great interest, consists of Constant's writings about literature. The most significant among them relate to tragedy, on the one hand, and to Mme. de Staël's writings on the other. One could add several literary analyses that appeared in *La Religion.*

4. Constant also left a considerable body of memoirs and autobiographical work, mainly published after his death. *Souvenirs historiques* and *Lettre sur Julie* came out during his lifetime. Posthumously, we have *Mémoires de Juliette, Mémoires inédits* (dictated) and, especially, two autobiographical accounts — *Cécile* (published for the first time in 1951), relating in barely disguised terms the history of his relationship with Charlotte, and *Ma Vie* (published in 1907), devoted to the first twenty years of his existence.

5. Constant's exclusively literary writings are few. In this category we have one tragedy, *Wallstein* (1808), adapted from Schiller, an epic and satirical poem, *Le Siège de Soissons* (1813-1814) and, of course, the short

novel *Adolphe,* first drafted in 1806, then altered and published in 1816. This was long regarded as a thinly disguised autobiography, an interpretation that has become inadmissible today.

6. Finally come the personal writings, letters and diaries, which were never intended for publication. Still, we must distinguish some degrees in that privacy. Certain letters, addressed to confidants like his cousin Rosalie Constant or his friends Prosper de Barante and Claude Hochet, contain passages that are repeated from one letter to another and that would have been publishable (political opinions, travel impressions, literary analyses); other letters, of love or self-analysis, may have just one recipient. Among the *Journals*, too, one holds a special status (perhaps it was revised); and it bears a title, *Amélie et Germaine* (1803). The others are strictly private and some of them are even written in code (1804-1807 and 1811-1816). These *Journals* have been known since the end of the 19th century, but were published in their entirety only in 1952.

Publication of the first edition of *Oeuvres complètes de Benjamin Constant* was begun in 1993, in Tübingen, Germany; it will consist of approximately forty volumes (four have appeared to date).

How Should Constant Be Read?

One of Constant's favorite formulas, which turns up many times under his pen, is: "In nature, everything fits together." Does his work illustrate this maxim? Does it have a unity and, if so, what kind? We should recall that, playing on his name, certain contemporary and posterior commentators have made much of the "inconstancy" of our author. They try to present him as a veritable weather vane, in his convictions as in his life. However, thanks to the publication of his previously unpublished writings, we know today that this is not the case. Constant himself characterizes his personality as "fluid," but this is not inconstancy; rather it is an extreme sensitivity to the elements of the context in which each experience occurs. As regards his ideas, it is, on the contrary, the great continuity that is striking. That is what made it possible for Constant to devote forty years to his work on religion and to publish without further editing political texts written 25 years earlier. Certain changes were made, but their scope was limited.

However, continuity over time is one thing, coherence in simultaneity is another. The difficulty here lies in the multiplicity of registers and fields in which Constant practiced. Even without searching for common themes everywhere, can one affirm that the coexistence of these various works makes sense?

It is the ambition of this essay to answer that question; not to propose a new biography, to analyze in detail such and such work nor, finally, to register Constant's thought in its historical context; but only to embrace in one single view the whole of Constant's activities, to try to reveal the overall schema. And we hasten to add that, the wealth and the complexity of Constant's work being what they are, this can only be a question of one course among other possibilities. Thus, we will consider at the same time Constant's political writings and his works about religion, and his novel and his autobiographical texts, and we will remember his political commitments as well as his experiences in love. The inclusion of all these modes of expression inside one and the same framework requires some clarification.

The framework is that of Constant's thought, not that of his life or of the formal characteristics of his works. However, some of his writings are not presented as the exposition of a thought. Constant left a philosophical doctrine, generalized and abstract, on political and religious life; he did not theorize on intimate life. To illuminate his views in that sphere, we must turn to his novel and his autobiographical writings, his diaries and his letters. The status of these texts is obviously not the same as that of the philosophical and historical works. Would we be correct to regard them on the same level? Sometimes, Constant seems to discourage us. Faithful, in that, to the spirit of his time, which we usually describe as "romantic," he states that any conceptual analysis would be out of place here:

> All our intimate feelings seem to make a mockery of the efforts of language: the words rebel, by generalizing that which they express, and serve to designate, to distinguish, rather than to define. Instruments of the mind, they render well only the notions of the mind. They fail at everything that has to do with, on the one hand, the

> senses, and on the other, the heart *(Religion,* I, I, 1, 35; *cf. Adolphe,* II, 18).

On other occasions, however, Constant allows for the possibility of analyzing the intimate world, on the condition that suitable means are found. A passage from the 1806 *Principes de politique* defines the difference between the two domains in this way:

> In the present state of society, personal relations are composed of fine nuances, undulating, impossible to grasp, which would be denatured in a thousand ways if one tried to pin them down with greater precision. Opinion alone can reach them (XVI, 8, 443).

It is no longer language in general that "personal relations" elude, but the language of "principles," as used by Constant in the course of that work; on the other hand, they remain accessible to "opinion." Again, Constant maintains that "common reason cannot satisfactorily explain any of the [passions]," *(Religion,* I, I, 1, 32) and that feelings are "inexplicable to the rigor of reason" (33). But these formulas do not preclude all hope, since man has tools at his disposal other than common and rigorous reason. He can approach this world by means that are well-known to literature: the image, the metaphor, the symbol, on the one hand; tales of specific instances, on the other. Elsewhere, Constant will be more precise.

The entire universe addresses mankind in an unspoken

> language that is understood in the interior of his heart,
> in a part of his being unknown to him, and which has
> both senses and thought [. . .] Why this intimate com-
> motion, which appears to reveal to us that which com-
> mon life obscures? Reason, clearly, cannot explain it;
> when it analyzes it, it disappears, but that is precisely
> why it lies essentially in the domain of poetry *(Guerre de
> Trente Ans,* 866).

Similarly, "observation of the human heart" is
Constant's explicit aim in his novel *Adolphe*
("Foreword" of the second edition, 6).

"Reason," in other words abstract argumentation,
is poorly suited to analysis of feelings or the inner
world; but "poetry" and literature are on their home
terrain. Constant takes up and expands upon the ideas
of the Encyclopedists, according to whom "opinion"
was a legitimate form of knowledge, halfway between
rigorous science and renunciation, a mode that is particularly appropriate to human realities. And, we
might add, the analysis of specific cases, such as the
ones we find in personal writings, are equally effective
in this.

Constant was no less lucid on his intimate life than
on political life, but he did not simply use the same
means to explore these different spheres of human existence. To be able to discuss political life and intimate
life inside the same framework, we are however compelled partly to transform the presentation of Constant
and to consider the whole of his works at the level of
"principles," to use one of his favorite terms. We are

not betraying Constant in so doing; as he explained in one of his first publications, *Des réactions politiques* (1797), it is essential to make the analysis abstract in order to get beyond questions of individual personalities and to allow for debate. Principles are not metaphysical fictions; rather they represent, for him, a theoretical practice. "Theory is nothing but practice reduced to a rule, through experience, and practice is nothing but applied theory" (*Principes*, I, 652). A purely abstract reflection is somewhat arbitrary; but, on the other hand, observation alone is not enough. Then one risks staying at the level of "a sterile study of isolated phenomena, an enumeration of effects without causes" (*Conquête,* "Appendice," 2, 264). Even if we have to take a different approach to each of the two domains, public and private, we must identify the relationship between the principles that govern them.

A second clarification relates to the status of personal writings and unpublished autobiographical work. Here we should recall that, although he devoted a great part of his time to the exploration of his own person during the middle period of his life, between 1800 and 1816, Constant would publish a single line of self-analysis. (*Adolphe,* once again, is by no means an autobiography, even if one may enjoy discovering a personal reminiscence, here and there). The memoirs that he publishes concern those events in which he plays a marginal role. In this respect, his attitude differs from those of Montaigne and Rousseau, who deliberately choose to make their own lives and persons the object of their public writings. The reasons Constant gives for his choice have to do with the vanity implied by any public discourse about oneself. "I am not interested enough in my life to take up other people's time with it," he writes at the beginning of his *Souvenirs historiques,* "and it would be impossible for me to say, like a well-known general (Dumouriez): 'While France was on fire, I was nursing a cold deep in Normandy.' " (72) He is more negative still at the end of *Adolphe:* "I hate that form of vanity shown by people who describe all the harm they have done, all the while asking everyone to feel sorry for them" ("Réponse," 83). Talking about oneself, even negatively, is a pleasure. The very act of making a statement has an element that is stronger than the content of the statement; saying to others, "I am suffering," is a pleasure greater than any suffering. To have others feel sorry for oneself is to flatter one's ego. The abandoned preface to *Adolphe* is equally severe. "In continually observing and describing himself, he believed he was making himself superior to himself, and managed only to overcome his good qualities" (196).

These analyses could have been signed by La Rochefoucauld; but La Rochefoucauld left only one brief self-portrait. By contrast, Constant dedicated most of his life and his efforts, until his fiftieth year, to self-analysis, even if he keeps the outcome of these analyses only for his closest relations. Thus we cannot ignore it, especially as he has clearly noted the absence of a distinct boundary between "writing for oneself" and "writing for others;" language being common to everyone, as soon as the feeling or the thought is formulated in words, the others are already present:

> When I started this [the diary], I made it a rule to write down everything that I experienced. I observed that law as best I could, and nonetheless such is the influence of speaking for the gallery that sometimes I did not observe it completely. How strange people are! One can never be completely independent.

Through the intermediary of language, "the gallery," the public, is within us, and one does not escape from other people by snuggling up with one's diary; complete independence is a futile dream. Perfect transparency is impossible in itself because, between the party having something to communicate and the party with whom he is communicating, there always stands the obstacle or the mediation of language. We speak using other people's words (from the past), and we speak to address ourselves to other people (into the future).

Does Constant, in his autobiographical writings, describe the singular individual that he is, or the man of his times, or even man in general? He himself wonders: "Are the others what I am? I don't know. Certainly, if I were to show them what I am, they would believe me insane. But if they were to show me what they are, would I perhaps believe them insane as well?" (*Journal*, December 18, 1804). He returns to this a few years later. "Does everyone have this feeling, and do they hide it as

I hide it? Does everyone play his part and make himself appear common and incoherent out of fear of seeming to be insane?" (to Prosper de Barante, April 22, 1808). Vanity tricks us into believing that others are not like us; to outsmart it, and until proven otherwise, it is better to carry on as though the truth of 'I' extends to other people.

Finally, a last clarification relates to how we will use Constant's biography. The biography as the identity of the person can explain why the author says this rather than that, what is the source of such and such assertion. But mostly we will put the author's biography to a different use; we will regard it as one form of expression among others. We are approaching Constant's thought by several avenues, for this thought is expressed by several means: written works and life experiences, literary writing and the sequence of events. The life is then no longer an explanation of his work but is itself a work that is particularly eloquent.

Liberal Democracy

Autonomy and Moderation

Constant's political thought can be presented as a synthesis and a transformation of the two major currents of 18th century French political philosophy, that of Montesquieu and that of Rousseau. The very first sentence of his great treatise *Principes de politique* refers to both *L'Esprit des lois* and to the *Contrat social*. Both these famous predecessors reflect upon the nature of the best political regime; but they do not see it in the same way.

For Montesquieu, it is not the number of people who hold power that matters (monarchy, aristocracy, democracy), but the way in which power is wielded. In his eyes, power is legitimate when it is not unlimited. One can limit it either by laws or by another power. Montesquieu thus wants the government to be subject to existing laws, and for the executive, legislature, and judiciary powers not to be concentrated in the same hands, so that one can counterbalance the other. If these precepts are followed, the result is a "moderate" or, as we would say today, liberal, regime. It does not matter much whether it is a monarchy or a republic; the moderate regime is, in itself, good. In the contrary case, the regime is despotic, and despotism must be fought always and everywhere.

Rousseau reasons in very different terms. For him autonomy is essential, i.e. whether an action is the result of its subject's will, in other words, whether one lives under laws that one has given oneself. Descartes required that reason not be subject to any external authority; Rousseau transposes this requirement to the political field and he declares: only that government is legitimate that has us live according to the law that we ourselves wanted. It is not how power is exercised that makes it good, but the way in which it is instituted. Monarchy is founded by tradition; but tradition can be only the result of a past injustice and it is always the effect of force, not of what is right. Only the republic is legitimate, in that here it is the sovereign people that decides the law according to which it will live.

Constant initially accepts Rousseau's postulate without hesitation: power must be the expression of the people's will; the good political regime is democratic. "In a word, there are only two powers in the world. One is illegitimate; that is force. The other is legitimate, and that is the general will" *(Principes,* 1806, I, 2, 22). But he is not satisfied with that and adds a constraint that takes Montesquieu as its starting point. It is not enough that power should be legitimate in its origins; it also must be exercised legitimately — in other words, it must not be unlimited. "When this authority extends over objects outside its sphere, it becomes illegitimate" (II, 2, 50). In other words, Constant adds together Rousseau's and Montesquieu's requirements for the best political regime. It must be both instituted *and* exercised in a certain manner, the general will having to be applied with moderation. The best regime is neither democracy nor liberalism, it is liberal democracy.

A synthesis of Montesquieu's and Rousseau's stipulations, Constant's thought is at the same time a criticism addressed to both. Rousseau, giddy with the discovery that political autonomy is possible, forgot or did not foresee a probable complication, to wit, that the autonomy of the community enters into conflict with the autonomy of the individual. The regime resulting from the French Revolution was quite democratic in that it derived from the sovereignty of the people; however, it was also a regime that could become despotic, as demonstrated by the Terror. This historical fact revealed a weakness in Rousseau's reasoning. It is not sufficient to require that the people be sovereign, still it must be specified that this sovereignty extends only up to a certain limit and not beyond. Indeed, the people, as legitimate sovereign, can exert a terror worse than that of the illegitimate monarch. "The people that is all-powerful is as dangerous as, or more dangerous than, a tyrant" (I, 6, 38). Thus it is necessary to build a wall that stops the general will at the edge of the individual's private territory and ensures the latter's protection.

> Democracy is authority deposited in the hands of all, but only that sum of authority necessary for the security of the group [. . .] The people can give up this authority in favor of just one man or a small number, but their power is limited, like that of the people who gave them this mantle (I, 7, 41).

Sovereignty is total only within certain bounds. Even if there is just one individual in dissension with all the others, these latter should not be able to impose their will upon him in his private life.

On the other side of this boundary begins the private space, where the individual alone is master. In disagreement with Rousseau, here Constant discovers an insurmountable heterogeneity within the social body. The individual cannot be reduced to his society; the principles that one and the other proclaim do not form a continuum. Constant cannot accept what Rousseau calls "the total alienation to the whole communityof each associate with all his rights" (*Le Contrat social* I, 6, 360). That the source of power is legitimate by no means prevents abuse. The reason for Rousseau's error is, according to Constant, in the abstraction of his system — he forgot that, in practice, the general will will be deposited in the hands of just a few individuals, and that this fact makes possible all forms of abuse. "In giving oneself up entirely, one does not enter into a condition that is equal for all, since some benefit exclusively from the sacrifice of the others" (*Principes*, 1806, I, 4, 34).

However, Montesquieu's solution, which requires that power be limited by laws and by other powers, is not enough for Constant either. Power may be distributed between distinct entities (the legislature, the executive and the judiciary) in vain. If their sum deprives me of a private territory, then I cannot approve such a regime:

> What matters to me is not that my personal rights cannot be violated by one power, without the approval of another; but that this violation should be prohibited to all the powers. It is not enough that the executive agents need to appeal for authorization by the legislator, it is essential that the legislator be able to authorize actions only within a given sphere (II, 3, 54).

Montesquieu says all the power should not be given into *the same hands,* Constant retorts: *all* the power should not be given away. Montesquieu takes care to make sure that power will stop power. Constant asks: "How can we limit power other than by power?" (II, 4, 55), and he answers: by establishing a territory on which no societal power, legitimate or illegitimate, divided or unified, has any right — the territory of the individual.

At the same time Constant, who observed the Revolution from close at hand, knows that the law can be as tyrannical as governments. Nothing prevents those who have seized power from drafting laws that authorize them to terrorize the population. Iniquitous laws are not hypothetical, they really exist. Therefore, a standard is needed that makes it possible to judge the laws. Constant recovers here the spirit of modern natural rights, which was present but veiled in Montesquieu's thought. Which characteristics make a law contrary to people's rights? Constant enumerates three of them: retroactivity; the prescription of actions contrary to morals, such as the refusal of compassion, or denunciations; and finally, collective responsibility, under which one could be punished for actions that one did not oneself commit. If laws do not transgress these principles, it is better to obey them, even when one may not agree with them. Order is preferable to disorder. But if they do contravene these principles, civic disobedience is not only licit, it is required. "Nothing excuses the man who lends his support to the law that he believes to be iniquitous" (XVIII, 6, 484). Constant would have no difficulty understanding the concept of a crime against humanity, an act that might be allowable under the laws in force but that transgresses the principles of rights and morals, the underpinnings of any law.

If obedience to positive laws and the separation of power are not enough, by what means can we ensure that freedom will be maintained? Above all, by establishing a fundamental law or constitution that states and specifies the possible extent of all the laws and all the powers; after that, by vigilance at every moment to ensure that the constitutional principles are not abrogated in practice. Certainly, this is why the writing of constitutions, and reflecting upon them, is one of Constant's passions — as testified by some of his works such as *La Constitution républicaine, Réflexions sur les constitutions et les garanties, Cours de politique constitutionnelle,* and *l'Acte additionnel* (a supplement to the Constitution) intended for Napoleon during the Hundred Days. This is also why, every time circumstances allow it, he participates in the country's political life.

Constant invents neither the democratic (or republican) principle of the sovereignty of the people nor the liberal principle of the limitation of power. Nonetheless it is he who articulates them, who holds them up against the real-life experience of the Revolution, the Empire, and the Restoration, who thus gives flesh to abstractions. It is he who reveals their consequences and sometimes their dangers. Constant is one of the first, and one of the most brilliant, authors who chose, among all the options that arose at the time, the one that appears to us today to be obvious (even if we are far from fulfilling it in all its perfection) — Revolution without Terror, popular sovereignty with respect for personal freedoms. In this, he is the first French theorist of liberal democracy.

The Principle of Freedom

And what is personal freedom? Constant's ideas on the subject were fixed since 1806; he would only revisit them and reformulate them over the rest of his life. Perhaps the simplest definition is the following.

"Freedom is nothing more than that which individuals have the right to do and that which society does not have the right to prevent" (*Principes*, 1806, I, 3, 28). Any human being's existence is divided into two domains, one public, the other private; one in which society exerts control, the other governed by the individual himself. *Freedom* is the name given to the border separating these two domains, to the barrier beyond which any intervention of society is illegitimate, where the individual decides everything by himself.

This is the point to which Constant returns most often, this is what he himself considers the leitmotiv of his political philosophy — the territory of the individual is not subject to societal sovereignty, whatever form that may take. When he tallies up the results of his battles, at the end of his life, in the foreword of his *Mélanges de littérature et de politique*, he repeats, "I defended the same principle for forty years, freedom in everything: religion, philosophy, literature, industry, politics" (519). Only "industrial" freedom (that is, that of productive labor) was added along the way. At this time, indeed, Constant thinks that competition must be permitted and the entrepreneurial spirit should not be regulated. The activity of production deserves these considerations, for it inherently belongs to the individual, as opposed to goods passed along through heritage. "The real estate asset is the value of the thing; the industrial one, the value of the man" (521).

In the *Principes* of 1806, the enumeration is a little different. Four subdivisions are found: 1. Freedom of action; 2. Freedom of conviction (or religious freedom); 3. Freedom of expression; and 4. Physical guarantee (one must be treated in accordance with the laws) (II, 6, 58). No limitation must apply to anything that is internal — no civil religion as in Rousseau. Such is also the conclusion of the work on religion. "Men, that is, those in power, the material force, must not interfere with religion" (*Religion*, V, XV, 4, 206). In this respect, Constant's vast study follows a construction parallel to that of his political treatises. The "Montesquieu" aspect is still visible here (for some time Constant wanted to call his great work *L'Esprit des religions*). In politics, as we have seen, it is not the opposition between one and many, monarchy and republic, that matters (Constant would defend the latter in 1800, the former in 1815), but that between limited and unlimited power. In the same way, in religion, the difference between polytheism and monotheism counts less, actually, than that between "sacerdotal" and "nonsacerdotal" religion, that is, containing or not containing a clergy, and thus also participating or not participating in political power. The first is, indeed, potentially "despotic," in that it can lead to a concentration of all the power in the same hands; the second, by contrast, is intrinsically "moderate."

Freedom of the press is also complete, except for that which harms the integrity of the person (slander, incitement to violence) or of the community (appealing to the population or to a foreign enemy to overthrow the ruling power). These exceptions do not justify the institution of censorship since, as infringements of the general law, they will be punished by that general law.

This segregation of freedom into various types is further refined, in other contexts, into additional segments. One can distinguish the pact between the government and the governed, which provides the guarantees of personal freedom, and the exercise of this freedom, or enjoyment. Absence of the former, notes Constant, would destroy the latter. From another perspective, one might also speak of a "moral freedom, which consists of making us independent of the passions that degrade us" (*Liberté politique,* 258). The latter is no longer identified with the protected territory of societal supervision, but with an internal purification; nevertheless, it benefits from personal freedom.

However, the most telling distinction is still to come. That is the distinction between the freedom of the individuals thus described and a very different form of social action, which consists of participating in the political life of one's country, which signifies another meaning of the word "freedom." To indicate this new contrast, Constant sometimes speaks of civil freedom and political freedom, or even of negative freedom and positive freedom, or again, as in his talk at the Atheneum in 1819, of the liberty of the Moderns and that of the Ancients.

Constant starts with a simple historical observation. Not every people recognized the same ideal of personal liberty; it has existed, actually, only since the

16th and especially the 18th century *(Liberté politique,* 257). The ancient Greeks, in particular, had no place for it; they were not concerned with preserving a space where the individual would decide everything by himself, because for them, "the individual was entirely sacrificed to the ensemble" *(Principes,* 1806, XVI, 1, 419). On the other hand, they cultivated a very different form of freedom, "active participation in collective power" *(Conquête,* II, 7, 164). "The aim of the Ancients was to share social power among all the citizens of a fatherland. That is what they called freedom *(liberté).* The aim of the Moderns is the security of private pleasures; and they call freedom the guarantees granted to these pleasures by social institutions" *(Liberté,* 502). For the Ancients, the individual is entirely subject to society; for the Moderns, it is society that must be put to the service of the individuals. The freedom of the Ancients is thus connected to the general will of Rousseau; that of the Moderns, to social moderation according to Montesquieu.

Where does this distinction between the Ancients and the Moderns originate? The quarrel by the same name was, itself, already old at that time, but the meaning of the distinction had changed. In Rousseau, one finds the intellectual articulation but not the terms: the Ancients, for him, are *citizens,* i.e. parts of a whole, "fractional unities"; the Moderns become, in the best case, *men,* that is, each one an individual, "an absolute entirety" *(cf. Emile,* I, 249). But Constant's immediate

45

source (and Mme. de Staël's — both share the same political ideas) is Condorcet. He already defends a concept similar to liberty: the majority, even if it is legitimate, should not be able to encroach on the territory of
the individual; now, only the Moderns discovered this
principle. "The Ancients did not have any concept of
this kind of liberty," writes Condorcet (*Oeuvres*, VII,
202). It is in this distinction and in this debate that the
modern idea of the individual is born.

The
"Era of the Individual"

The Virtue of Liberty

This new role of the person, with his private world where he reigns as Master, appears so essential to Constant that, when he looks for a name adapted to modern times, he spontaneously comes up with the "Era of the individual" (*Histoire abrégée de l'égalité,* 389). He considers that the development that brought the European peoples (the only ones that really arouse his interest) to this point is, on the whole, positive. They had arrived at a time when the collective body — be it the State, the corporation or the family — cannot dictate the behavior of the individual anymore. "Instead of the individual being controlled by the family, itself melded into the State, each individual lives his own life and claims his freedom." There is no more unity of ideas, no more automatic social consensus, but that is an advantage, not a disadvantage. "The intellectual anarchy that is so deplored seems to me to represent immense progress of intelligence" (*Les Cent-Jours*, "Introduction" to the second edition, 71), for the search for truth has replaced the absolute truth guaranteed by authority, and this is very good. Superior in terms of values, the modern era also facilitates to the maximum the happiness of its subjects, for now "to be happy, men need only to be allowed perfect independence, regarding everything that touches on their occupation, their sphere of activity, their imaginations" (*Conquête*, II, 7, 166). Freedom is all that is required for the happiness of modern man, whose part Constant resolutely takes.

A man of his times, Constant sees the relationship of the individual with his society as a combat. Society aspires to control the individuals' private space; they must therefore fight to protect it. The result of the fight is either private happiness or individual tragedy. Thus, when Constant reflects upon the future of literature and more particularly of tragedy, he sees only one possible subject. It is "the action of society in its struggle with man, obstructing not only his passions but his nature, crushing not only his character, his personal inclinations, but the impulses that are inherent in any human being" (*Tragédie*, 903). Society, in the eyes of the individual (or Constant), is only a kind of obstacle, labeled variously according to the ages and regions: despotism, religion, laws, habits. "It makes no difference, at heart it is always society weighing on man and chaining him down" (904).

For Constant, the individual is inevitably a "victim" of society, which is set against him by "a million against one" (912-913). For the Moderns, social action occupies the place that Providence held in the tragedy of the Ancients. The plots of future tragedies, as imagined by Constant, all lean in the same direction. One shows a black slave fighting for his release; his adversary is "the iron-clad institutions, the regime of blood, the hanging judges, the pitiless masters, all that arsenal of a police force crushing a single unfortunate person, because his color is different" (914). Another refers to the persecution, torture and extermination of the Huguenots. A third, an anecdote drawn from Saint-Simon's *Mémoires,* illustrates the arbitrariness and violence of royal power that punishes insubordination by death. Constant is himself impressed by the monotony of his examples, and forbids himself from always painting society black. However, in the only other subject of tragedy that he cites, the conflict is no less violent; only here society rightly fights against the individual-tyrant. When, on another occasion, Constant wishes to denote what appears to him the purest example of "human misery," the story of certain Ann Hurle, condemned and executed in England for fraud, he describes the state of maximum forfeiture as that of being totally rejected by society; and this condition comes from the fact that the individual person "was crushed under the iron hand of an implacable society" (*Journal,* April 20, 1804).

Perhaps this essentially negative vision of society reveals a blind spot in Constant's political thought. One has the impression that, scalded by the experience of the Revolution and, beyond that, of royal despotism, he cannot conceive that the State may also be beneficial for the individual. What if evil comes, rather, from other individuals, and society with its institutions is the protective shield? Doesn't the individual flourish all the more in a society that not only ensures his invulnerability but also contributes to his wellbeing? And, on the other hand, is it really enough to allow individuals to manage their private lives, as we might understand them, for them to know happiness? Is a life entirely devoted to the private world the best conceivable life? There is room for doubt. But it should be said that Constant himself does not entirely adhere to this unconditional praise of the Moderns.

A Critique of Modernity

In the same text where he introduces the contrast between the freedom of the Ancients and that of the Moderns, *Les Principes de politique* of 1806, Constant establishes five differences between the two eras; and the advantages are not always on the same side. The Moderns enjoy personal freedom, but the Ancients took an active part in their city's government (and found their happiness in that). The Moderns enjoy repose. "Repose, and with repose, comfort, and to arrive at comfort, industry — that is the single aim toward which mankind moves" (XVI, 3, 423). The Ancients preferred war, which brought glory and social cohesion. *L'Esprit de conquête,* on the same topic, adds that for the Moderns, "in place of glory, it would be better to have pleasure, in place of triumph, plunder" (I, 3, 90). The Moderns are more compassionate, the Ancients, more firm. Lastly, the Moderns are more lucid but they lack the passion of the Ancients. "The Ancients had, above all, a complete sense of conviction. We have, in regard to almost everything, only hypocrisy in place of conviction" (*Principes,* 1806, XVI, 6, 430; *L'Esprit de conquête* adds: "a soft and fluctuating conviction," II, 7, 167). We doubt everything, are tired beforehand with any undertaking, do not believe in the strength of our institutions. "Domestic affections replace the great public interests" (*Principes,* 1806, XVI, 7, 433).

In his great treatise dedicated to the *Principes de politique,* Constant counters philosophers such as Rousseau (in *Le Contrat social*) and Mably, who would like us to return to the freedom of the Ancients. Thus he defends what is modern, even if he points out where it causes our weaknesses. But, in other texts, he no longer has this strategic interest and can give free rein to his concern about the other aspect.

First of all, it is not true that relaxation and the passive pleasures are the fastest road to happiness. Repose is preferable to threat, certainly, but by the same token, it does cause trouble.

> Work, need, dangers attach us to life by offering at every moment battles to wage, goals to reach; while re-

> pose, by leaving us to ourselves, makes us painfully
> aware of the vacuum of an easy happiness and the in-
> adequacy of what we have. In order not to succumb un-
> der the overwhelming burden, man needs to be forced
> by obstacles to forget the sadness of his destiny
> *(Religion,* IV, IX, 7, 80-81).

Perhaps to his misfortune, man cannot be satisfied with repose. And, moreover, does happiness really constitute his only aspiration? "Is it really true, then," wonders Constant in his lecture on freedom, "that happiness, whatever form it takes, is the sole aim of mankind?" That would be an incomplete view of human needs. The enjoyment of pleasures corresponds to our animal side, but we are not reduced to that alone. Pleasures are not enough to give life meaning, i.e. a goal; yet that is what we seek. Constant has a name for this goal. "It is not to happiness alone, it is to improvement that our destiny calls us" *(Liberté,* 513).

Improvement ("perfectionnement") means the good of the community as well as that of the individual, and not individual gratification. It means, in Constant's vocabulary, political liberty (that of the Ancients), and not only civil liberty (that of the Moderns), moral elevation and not only the enjoyment of pleasures. For that, it would be sufficient that society be kept in order; but maintaining law and order is not society's only goal.

> If, to maintain it, all the generous emotions are sacri-
> ficed, men are reduced to a state not very different from

> that of certain industrious animals, whose well ordered
> hives and skillfully built combs do not measure up to
> the beautiful ideal of mankind *(Dunoyer,* 547).

Let us not confuse men with honeybees.

> Let us reject these narrow systems that offer mankind
> only the goal of physical wellbeing. Let us not confine
> ourselves to this life, so short and so imperfect, monoto-
> nous and at the same time agitated, and which, circum-
> scribed in its material limits, is indistinguishable from
> that of animals (550).

This danger is not a pure theoretical fabrication: on
the contrary, it is the state of mind that Constant observes and deplores around him. "We live in a era
when everything that is not concrete, everything that
does not produce a material product, seems to be only a
mental game and a waste of time," he writes to his
cousin Rosalie (October 6, 1825). "Anything that is not a
steam engine is a daydream." There is, parallel to social
progress but heading in the opposite direction, a continuous movement of "degeneration," whose signs are
easily read in the current era. Their overall meaning is
the replacement of liberty by necessity and thus of individual action by the movement of the masses. Mankind
becomes "a mechanical species, that will necessarily act
in a given way in any given circumstance" (to Prosper
de Barante, autumn 1810).

That the Moderns are satisfied with civil liberty
thus becomes for Constant not a reason for satisfaction

but a source of concern and a matter for reproach. The lack of any enthusiasm, any courage, any patriotism is no distinction. In his very first political pamphlet, *De la force du gouvernemente actuel* (1796), Constant already touches on this topic, which he shares at that time with Mme. de Staël. "Repose is good, but inactivity is evil." "The lack of goals, interests and hopes other than narrow and personal ones" makes life futile; "there is always something drab, colorless, about things that are only self-referential." Each of us also needs to be carried away by enthusiasm and to be in return "electrified by the recognition of our equals" (*Force*, VII, 71-72). Moreover, this modern state of mind threatens the individual himself, and not only the group. In an abandoned draft foreword for *Adolphe,* Constant writes:

> I wanted to depict in *Adolphe* one of the principal moral ills of our century, the fatigue, the concern, the lack of strength, the perpetual analysis that associates an ulterior motive with every feeling and that thereby weakens them at their birth (196).

This moral depression strikes every sphere of life — love as well as religion and politics:

> We no longer know how to love, to believe, nor to want. Everyone doubts what he says, smiles at the vehemence of what he affirms, and rushes to the end of what he experiences. [. . .] As a result, Heaven no longer offers hope, nor Earth dignity, nor the heart refuge (197).

The diagnosis, we see, is grim; here, we are far from the image, suggested by certain commentators, of Constant as a naive partisan of modernity. Modernity is desirable and, at the same time, dangerous. One could of course take comfort in thinking that between two evils it is necessary to choose the lesser, and that the disadvantages of modern freedom (lack of vital force and exaltation) are in spite of everything far preferable to those of the freedom of antiquity (subjection of the individual). Modern people have the right to say to the firebrands of old (such as, in some respects, Napoleon), "You are bored in the idleness of peace; why should we care about your boredom?" *(Conquête*, II, 8, 131). The Greeks' passion is responsible for the superiority of their poetry, but this too requires the leisure of the enlightened leadership class, which, in its turn, depends on the system of slavery. "We prefer to have fewer poets, and no more slaves" *(Religion*, IV, XII, 8, 454). The Moderns, certainly, are tired, but this very tiredness is the result of accumulated experience and knowledge that is not to be regretted.

So there are consolations, and yet they are quite fragile. Of greater concern to the community than individual moral depression is the fact that, to be maintained, civil liberty requires a certain amount of political freedom. In other words, if everyone is engaged only in his own affairs, the tyrant can seize power; however, under tyranny, there is no more leisure to deal with one's own affairs: one is obliged to submit oneself and follow.

Having practiced only "domestic virtues," one for-
gets that their exercise presupposes a society that respects and protects them – something that not all societies do.

> Its natural effect [that of modern society] is to make
> each individual his own center. However, when each
> one is his own center, everyone is isolated. When every-
> one is isolated, there is nothing but grains of dust. When
> the storm arrives, dust becomes mud.   (I, "Préface,"
> XXXVII).

Being concerned only with his personal pleasures,
the individual ignores public affairs and tries to ignore
the misfortunes of others, forgetting that his own private wellbeing depends on the public wellbeing. "He
deserted the cause of the fatherland because he did not,
of course, want to jeopardize his daughter's
dowry" (XXXV); but if the country is in flames, isn't the
dowry threatened?   For Constant, this is no purely
imaginary danger — that is precisely what was happen-
ing under Napoleon, whose intention was to reduce society to a collection of isolated individuals:

> The art of governments that oppress citizens is to keep
> them apart and to make communication difficult and
> meetings dangerous (*Principes,* 1806, "Additions," 628).

The isolation of individuals is perhaps not an inevitable consequence of modernity, but it is definitely one of its possible consequences, which modern tyrants will seek to implement.

Thus one must not be satisfied with hoping that the storm will pass and that one may hold onto his personal pleasures. The Moderns themselves cannot be allowed to desert the public sector. This conclusion enables us to get a better fix on Constant's precise location in the interleaved history of thought and society. Shortly after the French Revolution, he was the first *modern critic of modernity.* This choice pits him against the two dominating points of view of his time. In contrast to the conservatives, whose spectrum extends from Bonald to Tocqueville, he never regrets the change that has taken place; he is an unapologetic Modern. But that does not lead him toward triumphalism. Immediately alert to the new threats that have just emerged — materialism, individualism, the loss of vital force — Constant undertakes to analyze them and at the same time to seek the means of protecting against them. From his first political pamphlet in 1796 to the foreword of his last great work, *De la religion*, published in 1824, Constant repeats the same message: Beware the tendency to turn inward to the private domain, do not be satisfied with the egoistic happiness that is accessible to everyone. We need something more, something that transcends the individual; and furthermore, if we remain focused on ourselves at the individual level, even that happiness will disappear. The public spirit, political freedom, must imperatively be maintained.

The three domains that were distinguished in the abandoned foreword to *Adolphe* will be the three domains inside of which Constant will exert his critical and constructive spirit: the political and social world of public action, the realm of our will and of dignity; the intimate life of affection and love; and religion, in which the visible is linked to the invisible, and by means of which man turns toward God. To understand which are the specifically modern threats that affect politics, love and religion, to find a way around them without giving up the modern identity itself — such will be the intellectual and militant plan that will animate Constant in all his activity.

Historicism or Essentialism

Inexorable History

And now it is our turn to explore the three domains distinguished by Constant — politics, love and
religion — to observe the dangers that he describes and
to examine the remedies that he proposes. First, we
must return to what he himself judges to be the focal
point of his analysis, the liberty of the Moderns. In the
sense that Constant uses this term, liberty is not an eternal value but a characteristic of individualistic societies,
such as contemporary European societies. Constant
seems to have absorbed the relativistic and structural
lessons of Montesquieu: a society is a system that en-
compasses everything, the climate and the national
spirit, the laws and the manners. Any thing can be
good, "provided that it is the natural result of the situation and of the character of the people [. . .] All things
human [. . .] are [. . .], in their time, good and useful.

Taken out of context, they are all disastrous" (*Principes*, 1806, XIII, 1, 333-334). The differences between individuals belonging to specific societies in history are comparable to the differences between animal species (*Conquest*, I, 15, 131-2). This historical relativism is the consequence of the temporal dimension of mankind — change is an inherent characteristic of mankind. "Everything that has to do with man and his opinions on any topic whatsoever is necessarily progressive, i.e. variable and transitory" (*Idées religieuses*, 523). In this, Constant remains faithful to the principles of Rousseau, too. Man's nature is not established once and for all; he can become something that he never was before — but man has a history and is acquainted with the multiplicity of cultures.

Not only do institutions and opinions depend on the time and place where they are formulated but moreover, states Constant, the force of this determinism is insurmountable. Absolute necessity reigns over the history of human societies (this thesis, which has become a banality by the end of the 19th century, was an innovation at the time of Constant's writing). "A century is the necessary result of those that preceded it. A century can never be anything but that which it is." So there is something ridiculous in wishing to pass judgement on what has gone before. "There is nothing there to censure nor to praise. [. . .] The spirit of a century is a necessary fact, a physical fact. And a physical fact is to be stated and not judged" (*Littérature du XVIIIᵉ siècle*, 528).

Not necessarily consciously, individuals participate in the spirit of their time. "All things human follow a progressive path, independent of men, and which they obey without knowing it. Their very will is included, because they can never want but what is in their interest and because their interest depends on the coexistent circumstances" (*Polythéism*, II, XIV, 3, 168; perhaps we should recall that these last two texts, particularly "historicist," were not published by Constant himself). The best attitude to hold thus seems to be acceptance of this determination:

> If the path mankind follows is invariable, one must submit. Resignation alone will save men from foolish struggles and dreadful misfortunes" (*Pensées détachées*, 603; cf. OC, III, 1, 445).

Writers, in particular, think that the ideas they formulate are found within themselves, and believe they influence their contemporaries and their age; and in this they succumb to a pleasant illusion. "Writers are only the organs of the dominant opinions. Their agreement with these opinions, their fidelity in expressing them is the foundation of their success" (*Religion*, I, I, 2, 43). How could it be otherwise? "No individual, young or old, shakes off the yoke of his century," Constant writes in connection with Homer. "The impressions of the atmosphere that surrounds us become part of us; they become part of our existence; every part of us is penetrated" (*Religion*, III, VIII, 2, 434-435). Those who thought they were shaping their century are, at best, eloquent spokesmen. "They appear to be moving it along, because they serve it; they appear to be its guides because they are its interpreters; they appear to persuade it because they reveal its own secrets to itself" (*Littérature du XVIII*ᵉ *siècle*, 528).

The March Toward Equality

This determinism is not diminished by the application of universal categories of evaluation, even if they do temper the relativism that is sporadically proclaimed. Indeed Constant thinks that *equality* is, as far as the life of societies is concerned, one such value. Men are not equal among themselves, and without protest they accept institutional inequalities that are part of tradition. But they all have inside themselves, without anyone having to inculcate it, an ideal of justice that holds that under equal conditions, each one must be dealt with in the same manner. That feeling is innate and universal. "Equality is thus an abstraction built on antecedents that violated it or accidents that disturbed it, the primitive law; and the desire for equality is the most natural of our feelings" (*Histoire abrégée de l'égalité*, 370). "Love of equality is a passion ignited deep in our hearts by nature" (373). In its turn, "justice is nothing but equality invested with the force of law" (372). This must be understood clearly — it does not mean that everyone should receive the same treatment, but that everyone should be judged according to the same principles, according to his merits. Equality "is distributive justice. It is not the absence of any difference in social advantages" (*Filangieri*, IV, 6, 401). This equivalence between justice and equality is, for men, "a natural effect of their reciprocal relations" (*Education*, 576); it arises from their sociability itself.

If the equality thus understood is a universal and eternal value, that means that we have an instrument by which the various regimes and political institutions can be judged. We can judge the past, instead of being satisfied to recount it. Legalized immorality, injustice, arbitrary judgement are contrary to nature, and contrary to Constant's declarations elsewhere. "I withhold my respect for the past only in the case of those things that are unjust," he writes — but is this not a large exception? "Time does not sanction injustice. Slavery, for example, is not legitimated by elapsed time" (*Conquête*, I, 13, 120). That means, moreover, that the term "improvement" has a precise meaning. It means, for a society, to approach ideal equality. "The perfectibility of mankind is nothing but the tendency toward equality" (*Perfectibilité*, I, 591). Liberty itself, which we have seen has only a historical value (nobody could imagine modern freedom among the Ancient peoples) regains an absolute meaning as a means for improvement, that is, for approaching equality:

> Freedom is especially precious because it ensures the examination and the appreciation of opinions, and because it leads by this means to the correction of ideas, to the reform of abuses, to the improvement of morals

(*Constitution républicaine*, VIII, 10, 416-417).

Equality is thus an absolute value that escapes general historicism; but it also constitutes the goal and, consequently, the direction of history. Indeed, Constant believes that history moves in a certain direction, progressing from imperfection toward perfection, and that it is inexorable even if, in detail, it seems to move like a pendulum. In other words, he is not satisfied to propose equality as a universal value, as a category of the spirit making it possible to consider the most varied facts; he believes that equality, or rather progress toward it, is an integral part of reality. He is, in this respect also, a disciple of Condorcet (the Condorcet of *Progrès de l'esprit humain*) and of Lessing (as in *Die Erziehung des Menschengeschlechts* [The Education of the Human Race]). Humanity in its evolution follows the road to progress, that is, to reconciliation with equality; which also means that Constant's thought, in terms of values, far from diluting all absolutes in history, submits history to the system. His most general manuscript on this subject bears a significant title: *Du moment actuel et de la destinée de l'espèce humaine, ou Histoire abrégée de l'égalité* [On the Present Time and the Destiny of the Human Species, or an Abridged History of Equality]. Mankind's destiny is nothing but its march toward equality. This draft of Constant's did not come to fruition, which is hardly astonishing, but its author made use of the distinctions that he established there in his

other writings, in particular those dedicated to religion. The great stages of human history, each characterized by a higher form of equality, would be called:
savagery; theocracy; slavery; feudalism; nobility;
succeeding at the present time to what we must undoubtedly call democracy (cf. *Idées religieuses*, 523 s.).

This faith in progress is the most irrational element in Constant's thought (even if the past had followed a movement of progress, that would not prove
anything as to the future) and resembles the faith
other people put in God. One might wonder, moreover: if the advent of progress were assured (by history or Providence, it does not matter which), what
good is it to strive and to deceive oneself on the role
of one's liberty? Perhaps Constant is not a relativist,
but rather shows himself here to be quite deterministic.

The result of this argumentation may be a surprise. Constant starts with a plea for liberty, the supreme value. Then he realizes that this value belongs to our modern time only; he adds, finally, that
any era determines entirely those who live in it, and
that the history of humanity corresponds to a pre-
established design. In other words, we are not free
to be free, we are free only by necessity. Constant reproached Rousseau for requiring that citizens be
forced to be free; but isn't he, by making liberty one
of the characteristics of our time (and of his time), an
implacable necessity, taking away from us with one

hand that which he so generously offers with the other?

The Unity and the Liberty of Mankind

That is incontestably a problem, but Constant has not ignored it. In a way, his work is an attempt to articulate these two separate requirements — to believe in a universal humanity, founded in liberty but, at the same time, to take into account the development of the various societies and the force of social pressures.

For man is one, whatever the stage of his development. "Whether man is savage or is organized, he has the same nature, the same primitive faculties, the same tendency to employ them" (*Religion*, I, II, 8, 367).

The "rash scorn that civilization lavishes upon the Savages" must be condemned (I, II, 2, 264), which means that even if everything is in flux, something remains stable. Men always live in society and society always has both a reality and an ideal, in other words a moral aspect; that is what makes men human.

In his work on religion, Constant sets out to distinguish between that which remains the same (and which characterizes the human species) and that which varies (his societies); like Kant, to separate the religious feeling, which is permanent, from its varying forms. "Religious feeling is an essential attribute, a quality inherent in our nature" (I, I, 7, 142). "The idea, or rather the sense of the Divinity, has existed in every era" (I, I,

9, 216). But its incarnation on earth is inevitably historical. "While the essence is always the same, immutable,
eternal, the form is variable and transitory" (I, I, 1, 26).
"Every epoch had its prophets and its men of inspiration, but each one spoke the language of his times. In
principle, there is nothing historical in religion, or in the
idea of Divinity; but everything is historical in the way
they are developed" (I, I, 9, 216).

It is history that obeys the momentum toward
equality, but there is also a trans-historic human identity (which includes, notably, religious feeling). The
great question is at what level the analysis is conducted;
if it is carefully defined, beyond the heterogeneity of the
facts one may catch a glimpse of the permanence of the
categories. The religious sensibility itself, we will see
later, is only one component of a broader domain, entirely characteristic of humanity as a species.

Moreover, Constant is careful to specify that even
when historical conditions determine the overall trend,
they leave to individuals an irreducible space of liberty:

> Everything is moral with individuals, but everything is
> physical with the masses. [. . .] Each one is free indi-
> vidually because he does not, individually, have to deal
> with anything but himself, or with forces equal to his.
> But as soon as he becomes part of a group, he ceases to
> be free *(Littérature du XVIIIe siècle, 528).*

The individual acts according to his will; his acts
can thus be evaluated on the moral plane. But, as mem-

bers of an ensemble — of people, of an era — individuals participate in a movement of which they may not necessarily be conscious: an invisible force leads them toward a goal of its own. The debate over liberty vs. determinism must be solved not by choosing one term over another but, again, by defining the levels at which they operate. At the level of the individual, liberty wins. The individual is responsible for each of his acts, for he has the choice of obeying or disobeying the natural and social pressures that he experiences. But if we focus less on individual acts and more on generalities, whether of a people or an era, and the less effect this liberty has, the more clearly we can perceive those forces that are beyond individual control. Certain eras, however, impose conformity and absorb the individual into the mass; by this means they deprive him of his essential freedom.

Thus it is not true that the individual is justified in abdicating his will under the pretext that no matter what he does, the result will be always the same. A thinker, in particular, would have no excuse for behaving this way. But, in truth, thought is never the pure product of circumstance, and writers have often found that a certain political freedom is also required in order to be able to express opinions contradicting the spirit of their time. Such is the example provided earlier by the Greek philosophers:

> Philosophers [. . .], although dominated like any individuals by the spirit of their century, and impelled by

> this spirit in the same direction, nevertheless enjoy an individual independence which introduces into their assumptions many variations and digressions almost impossible to calculate *(Polythéism,* I, V, 1, 145).

The same applies to modern sages such as Montesquieu. As a member of a group, the aristocracy, he often defends their interests quite predictably; but, as an authentic philosopher, he removes himself from this determination to serve not the collective interest, but the interest of the truth:

> His genius, and the bitterness inherent in genius, sometimes dictated words to him that struck down the very same abuses toward which his customs and social position inspired him to be partial and indulgent *(Filangieri,* I, I, 190).

It is something of this ideal, finally, that inspires Constant when he tackles his great work on religion. "We have tried to forget, while writing, the century, the circumstances and contemporary opinions," he affirms in his preface (I, XIX).

The Reign of Interest

One could summarize all the foregoing by saying that Constant never adheres to a single dogma, but that he begins by recognizing two forces, or two requirements, or two contrary needs, and that he seeks not to reconcile them but to articulate them. He is neither looking to substitute Rousseau's principles for Montesquieu's, nor the reverse, but is seeking how one can live with both, why and how one must call for both popular sovereignty and freedom of the individual. It would be a mistake to believe that Constant chooses the freedom of the Moderns over that of the Ancients. He describes the first with more ardor and sympathy than the second, but that is because it was previously ignored and because he is himself a son of his times. Nevertheless, he recommends a combination of both, not a choice of one or the other. The development that led to our modernity deserves both praise and blame; modernity must be viewed critically, but while remaining modern oneself. The universality and diversity of mankind, the absolute or relative character of value judgements, free or determined action — on each of these questions Constant encourages us not to choose one term to the detriment of the other, but to consider both simultaneously. They are not choices to be made but discrepancies that define the thought of man and his societies. Constant's attitude is not dogmatic but dialogical. He does not seek to close the debate with a simple and definitive answer, but to shake off initial certainty and lead us toward more enlightened convictions.

Interest as a Motive

We have not completely finished with Constant's political philosophy. Every society recognizes a division between private space and public space, even if the extent of the territories thus delimited varies over the course of history. The government's jurisdiction is perfectly legitimate inside its boundaries. Constant does not say, "Let us have as little government as possible," nor "government is a necessary evil." No; provided that it stays inside its territory, government is a good thing, and we should wish that it may be as strong as possible. "Government has a sphere which is proper to it.[. . .] It is thus not an evil, except to criminals, and it is good that it should be an evil to them" (*Godwin*, 565-566). Equality is the (universal) value that dominates the public space and provides the foundation for justice to be exercised; justice is not a private affair and must be rendered, even if the offended have forgiven their offenders. That being the case, one may still wonder, first, what values are at work in the private domain; and, second, what driving forces, other than values, govern these two spaces.

One of the great motives of human activity, private as well as public, is undoubtedly the pursuit of self interest. In his youth, Constant regarded as a disciple of Helvetius, who made the concept of interest the cornerstone of his philosophy. And, in his first doctrinal writings, for example in the work on *La Constitution républicaine,* Constant regularly refers to the need to take interest into account. The *general will* is directed by the common interest; and that, in its turn, is the combination of specific interests. Constant does not revel in great words without examining which specific realities they bring to us. For a political arrangement to be solid, it must correspond to the present interests. "These principles have their guarantee in the interest of the governments and the governed, and in the public spirit that is the product of this interest" (VIII, 11, 420). Throughout his lifetime, Constant would grant considerable weight to this driving force in human action.

> If interest is not the motive behind every individual (for there are individuals whose nobler nature raises them above the narrow concerns of selfishness), interest is the motive of all the classes *(Filangieri,* I, 5, 204).

In his diary, Constant gives many illustrations of this mainspring of human action: in order to observe it, one need only look behind the protagonists' stated motivations.

To act according to one's interest is a feature common to all men; so interest readily fits in with a theory inspired by the ideal of equality. It could never play a comparable role in the aristocratic world, founded upon a hierarchy that determines privileges and honors. To respect each one's interest is to grant the same dignity to each. That, however, is not sufficient to justify using this concept alone in the analysis of human conduct, in the manner of Helvetius or, before him, of La Rochefoucauld. From 1802 onward (the year during which Constant studied the work of Bentham, and utilitarian thought, which proclaims the concept of "a well-understood interest"), his references to interest as a motive are tempered with reservations. Interest is certainly present, but it does not explain everything. A general anthropology that is based on this single category is a lame anthropology. This is why Constant submits to critical analysis those who appear to him to be its promoters: Epicures among the Ancients (in *Polythéisme,* I, VIII, 1) and, among the Moderns, Helvetius himself (cf. *Religion,* I, "Préface," XXXI) and Bentham (in the 1806 *Principes*).

First, we should be clear about the meaning of the word. Certain authors have broadened its use until it included any benefit for the subject, however indirect that may be. According to this usage, one's interest could lie in the sacrifice of one's own wellbeing for that of humanity: that too, in a very general sense, is in the interest of the individual. But Rousseau had already warned against such an extension of meaning, which deprives the term of any discriminatory virtue. "Every one, they say, contributes to the public good in his own interest; but why then do the just contribute to their own detriment? What does it mean to go to one's death, in one's own interest? Undoubtedly, people act only for their own good; but if we do not take into consideration moral good, we will never explain by interest alone any but the actions of miscreants" (*Emile*, IV, 599).

Constant heartily agrees with this — we cannot speak of "interest" if my interest consists in giving others the advantage; the only true "interest" is that which serves my egoism directly, without being mediated by the idea of duty and without someone else being made the beneficiary:

> Well-understood interest? Miserable system, founded on an ambiguous absurdity, of necessity leaving passion to judge this interest, and putting on the same line and cloaking under the same name any calculation of narrowest selfishness and the most sublime devotion! (*Religion*, I, I, 3, 73).

Thus it is better to give up the use of so misleading a word as "interest" or "utility."

Then Constant criticizes doctrines based on personal interest on both moral and factual grounds. If one proposed that interest alone governs men, one would be obliged to give up all morality (*Principes,* 1806, II, 7, 6 1), but such a conclusion would be dangerous. The image that we have of ourselves influences our behavior; he who believes himself to be immoral becomes so. But if the only reasons to reject the doctrine lay in the undesirable consequences caused by adopting it, the doctrine would not have been abandoned because the principle would not have been judged on its own, but on the basis of its utility. Constant thus advances a second reason for refusing the absolute reign of interest — and that is that it does not explain a great part of human behavior, namely the faculty of the human heart "to be subjugated, to be dominated, to be exalted, independently of and even contrary to its interest" (*Religion,* I, "Préface," XXVI). Constant's usual examples illustrating this faculty are religious inspiration, love, enthusiasm, devotion; we will return to this later. Interest is considered here in the name of what man *is*, not of what he should be.

Time, and Other People

How can we explain human behavior that includes these disinterested actions? In one of his most philosophical texts, Constant places ideas above feelings. People are willing to sacrifice present sensations "for the hope of a future sensation, that is, for an idea" (*Perfectibilité*, I, 584). Since we are no longer satisfied with the present moment, we also use the considerations of our dependence with regard to other people and the world, which are no longer reduced to egoistic interest alone. All things considered, the only coherent version of the doctrine of interest would be the reduction of man to a pure consumer of immediate pleasures; however, that is obviously false. Man is aware of himself and his position in time, therefore also of his finitude. If one did not have to die, one might be tempted to live a life based only on interest, to accumulate and preserve the greatest number of benefits; but such is not the case.

> Death — which interrupts these calculations, which makes these successes futile; death which seizes power in order to dash it into the pit, naked and disarmed — is an eloquent and necessary ally of all the feelings that surge within us in this world (*Religion*, I, II, 4, 286).

Paradoxically, awareness of death makes the reign of interest, on its own, impossible. Moreover, one cannot conceive of man entirely isolated from other men. "A thousand bonds tie us to our peers, and the most anxious selfishness does not manage to break them all" (*Conquête*, II, 11, 187). Man thus feels the need for a double transcendence: in time (born of our awareness of death) and in space (founded on our necessarily social existence).

The theory of interest as the exclusive master is

false, but that does not prevent it from being very wide-spread. It even had a partisan of some stature — Napoleon himself. According to Constant, the Emperor's philosophy was reduced to that principle. Napoleon was "calculation personified" ("Appendice," 2, 259). "He did not look on men as moral beings, but as things" (*Les Cent-Jours*, II, 1, 206). "The conviction that mankind is devoted only to his interest, obeys only force, deserves only contempt;" that was, according to Constant, Napoleon's judgement on men (I, 6, 130). And Napoleon's politics were founded on this concept of mankind. "If there is only interest in the heart of man, tyranny needs only to frighten him or to seduce him in order to dominate him." But Napoleon alone is not responsible for this deleterious doctrine. It was already practiced and promoted during the 18th century by the absolute monarchy, follower of a naive "Epicureanism;" in addition, it was professed by the materialist thinkers of the Age of Enlightenment, who gravely affirmed that "man is motivated only by his interest." Finally, Napoleon was encouraged by the population itself, which liked to flatter those in power while expecting to be rewarded for doing so. The multitude "eagerly sought to be enslaved" (*Conquête*, "Appendice," 2, 260) and Constant was keenly aware that for twelve years he saw "only outstretched hands begging for chains" (*Les Cent-Jours*, II, "Huitième note," 303).

In the final analysis, the falseness of the theory

brought about Napoleon's downfall; at the same time, his downfall illustrates the falseness of the theory. "To know men, it is not enough to scorn them," Constant declares in a strong statement (*Conquête*, I, 14, 128). He goes against the mainstream of modern Western thought that would suggest that the truth is necessarily alarming: politics based only on self-interest breaks down, even if this ruin comes about only over time. Here we see hints of the role reserved for scholars and thinkers — that of criticizing and improving the common representations of man and society. Napoleonic tyranny is at least partially due to the success of the philosophical theories reducing man to a being subject to the reign of self-interest.

Constant's philosophical-political choice is defined by a double contrast, hidden in the dual meaning of the word "liberty:" the antithesis of traditional authority and, at the same time, of materialist causality. For, on the one hand, Constant remains an uncompromising partisan of each one's right to choose his own life, rejecting blind subservience to an arbitrary tradition. But, in addition, he is no less resolutely opposed to ambient determinism, which resulted from the materialism of the Enlightenment and found powerful support in the triumphant scientific spirit. According to this view, man is a solitary being, entirely subject to his material interests and determined by forces that transcend him. By rejecting both these points, Constant's position defines itself as that of a *humanist,* neither individualist nor communitarian, always attacked from both the left and the right, defending liberty against all its enemies.

Political Commitment

A Centrist Position

How well does Constant's engagement in public life illustrate his principles? Our author is not satisfied with elaborating doctrines; on several occasions in his life, he becomes a man of action. He is politically active before and after the Empire — between 1795 and 1802, then in 1814-1815, and finally from 1817 until his death in 1830. In his political life, Constant was sometimes reproached (during his lifetime as well as after) with having been an opportunist who, behind the declaration of noble principles, dissimulated the defense of his own interests. Was the doctrinaire liberal, in practice, an egoist and a Machiavellian? Constant was particularly persecuted in the 20th century by a polemist and a self-proclaimed historian, Guillemin. In works peppered with numerous references but where the quotations are cut short and taken out of context, he set out to prove that Constant had always acted only in his material interest, all his philosophical reflection being only a hypocritical mask pasted over his passion for money.

Several attentive historians, beginning with Beatrice Jasinski, have already demonstrated the weakness of these charges and the bad faith expressed by the polemist; we will not go into it again. The tone he adopted reveals in itself the excessive position he takes. How can we trust someone who, in the first pages of his book, cannot hide his physical repulsion toward "that squirming, lisping, bespectacled redhead;" he certainly does not tire of winding up "the thread inexhaustibly secreted by this spider." Mme. de Staël, lascivious of course, is hardly treated with more benevolence, and Mme. de Charrière is "an aging literary lady beginning to sour." Is scorn enough in order to know men? When the polemist can imagine only sordid motivations, he may be telling us more about himself than about those whom he abuses with such rancor.

Beyond the invectives and calumnies, we must examine the facts. One may point out as an example here two episodes in Constant's political life, in the course of which he might indeed be reproached for "inconstancy." His first contact with the political life of France occurs during the summer of 1795. The Thermidor Assembly (the national assembly following the overthrow of Robespierre) had to be renewed; certain deputies proposed that the assembly re-elect itself. In the month of June, Constant published his first political articles: he condemned this initiative, on behalf of the principle of political responsibility. However, in August of the same year, we find him collaborating with Louvet, the President of the Convention, to defend it against attacks on behalf of the royalists. Why this about-face?

One might be satisfied to observe that, in his first steps in political life, Constant lacked experience and made some missteps; what is exceptional in that? In June, freshly arrived in Paris, he initially sees the danger that the conventionists represent: self-perpetuating their assembly would be a major distortion of democratic principles. In August he is better informed and realizes that the very existence of the Convention, and thus of the Republic, is threatened by the royalist forces. He concludes, with reason, that an imperfect Convention is better than no Convention at all; at this specific moment, it should be defended rather than attacked. There is nothing sectarian about Constant; he is not one of those who know the answer to every question in advance. His knowledge influences his acts.

But this change of position also reveals a more important aspect of Constant's political commitment. His fundamental choice should be emphasized: Revolution without Terror, a popular sovereignty that does not override personal freedoms. Such a position is defined by two negatives: the rejection of those who are against the Revolution, and the rejection of those who want to push it to the point of Terror. Thus Constant's attitude is, from the start, that of a *centrist* who fights two extremes. This is why he must constantly turn from one front to the other and battle against arguments which are in conflict themselves; however, that does not put Constant in any contradictory position. In this case, centrism should be understood in the philosophical sense and not in terms of a party (when he was elected as a deputy, Constant would defend the liberals, i.e. "the left" of his time).

This is no reversal of principle; but Constant's ideas are a little more complex than the usual political credos. His attitude remains consistent before and after this date. Already in 1793, while observing from Switzerland the sudden upstarts of revolutionary France, he is ready to change party provided that his ideal is kept intact. "If the [foreign] Powers wanted to restore a government that is at least faintly moderate, I would jump to take sides with them" (to Mme. de Charrière, October 16-18, 1793). In the autumn of 1795, when the dangers to the Republic are accumulating, he still hopes that France will be able to dodge "the two extremes of royalism and terrorism" (to his aunt, the countess of Nassau, October 21, 1795).

Constant's "centrist" position, in politics as in philosophy, would be responsible for other latter day misunderstandings and would damage his reputation among those who like simple answers. Under the Restoration, he would still be obliged to fight on two fronts. On the one hand, he is against the extremists who want the return of the *Ancien Régime*, even the introduction of theocracy; on the other hand, he polemicizes with the adherents of deterministic materialism, who were recruiting among Napoleon's faithful as well as among those following the utopian socialism of Saint-Simon. This intermediate position undoubtedly explains why his work *De la religion* causes so many hostile reactions. Constant is too religious for the materialists, yet not enough the traditional Christian to please the devout. In France, he complained, "what is required is that an author attack or defend. The hell with anyone who only wants to judge!" (to Prosper de Barante, February 25, 1808). How can we categorize someone who has decided never to sacrifice nuances?

Individuals and Principles

Constant's "centrism" is not the only reason for his apparent ambivalence. On several occasions his relationship with Napoleon illustrates another aspect. In 1799, Constant wished to play a more active political role; thanks to Siéyès, and thus indirectly to Napoleon himself, he managed to be appointed to the Tribunat, a somewhat artificial institution where future laws were publicly discussed. However, scarcely appointed, Constant joined the opposition and became one of the most vigilant critics of Napoleonic efforts gradually to legalize the dictatorship; so much so that Napoleon required and obtained, after two years, his elimination from the Tribunat.

The other moment of direct contact with Napoleon is even more surprising; it happened during the Hundred Days. Napoleon disembarked at Golfe-Juan and headed for Paris. Constant, who was certainly no unconditional partisan of the Bourbons, was frightened at the prospect of the Emperor's return: a constitutional and moderate monarchy appeared to him preferable to a despotic empire. On March 19, 1815, he published a violently anti-Bonapartist article, in which one reads:

> I will not go, miserable defector, to drag myself from one power to another, to cover infamy by sophism and to stammer profane words to redeem a shameful life (*Article*, 150-1).

Fifteen days later, however, he is in the process of writing a constitution for Napoleon, who appointed him a member of the State Council. Three months go by, and Constant asks for pardon from Louis XVIII, who has returned to France.

Opportunism? Less than it seems. How are these about-faces explained? By a simple fact: Constant is loyal not to parties, but to principles. In that, his behavior lies within the scope of morals rather than in politics. In modern States, political commitment goes by affiliation with a party, which above all requires fidelity. However, Constant is not a party man: not because he is a saint (he is perfectly capable of taking his own interests into account), but because he extends his loyalty to the ideas in which he believes, not to the apparatuses. In 1799, in order to influence politics in France, one had to be part of the institutions; thus he readily accepts Napoleon's indirect assistance to reach the Tribunat. But, once in place, he does not feel encumbered by any gratitude nor obligation towards his "benefactor": he is there to defend what is right and just, not to serve specific interests. Napoleon does not understand; he is perplexed and furious. This young man was, to some extent, his protégé, he owes everything to him, he ought to have been at Napoleon's service; instead of which, the ingrate sets to work sticking a monkey wrench in his plans, throughout the two years he remains in the Tribunat!

The situation was similar in 1815, even if the roles are not the same. Constant is again faithful, not to individuals, but to principles (he wrote in his *Journal* during the Hundred Days: "I am going all out, full tilt, without abjuring any principles," April 19, 1815). He does not believe in an immutable identity of the person that would remain insensitive to circumstances; however, he always proclaims the same ideals. If he is defending the idea of a constitutional monarchy, it doesn't matter much to him whether the name of the monarch is Napoleon or Louis. Under Napoleon, he wrote the draft of a constitution more liberal and more coherent than that which was in force before. His *Principes de politique,* a very abbreviated version of the great 1806 treatise, would be published during the Hundred Days, in May 1815; the work is fundamentally hostile to the Napoleonic dictatorship of the latter years. The opportunist is not always the one we think it is. It is not Constant who changed, making the collaboration of the two men possible, it is Napoleon, who must have been even more perplexed this time. How is it possible that my former enemy now comes to my aid? And neither does the request for pardon, in the autumn of 1815, after the second abdication of Napoleon, imply a turnabout. People change, principles stay the same. Constant is ready to behave fairly with any monarch who engages to respect the constitution and fundamental freedoms. His fidelity to the same ideal is never contradicted; it is not his fault if the people around him change theirs.

Let us not misunderstand. In standing by political principles rather than by individuals, Constant does not choose abstraction in place of living people, he chooses an ideal rather than a party. That does not prevent him from defending individuals who, without agreeing with his political beliefs, were victims of injustices (for example, the royalist journalist Fiévée in 1818). He agrees completely with Mme. de Staël's choice – she, he remembers, had her own political preferences, but was equally ready to help the royalist and the revolutionary, however slightly they were threatened and persecuted.

> The sight of someone suffering reminded her that there
> was something in this world more sacred to her than the

success of a cause or the triumph of an opinion. [. . .]
Outcasts of every stripe found in her more zeal to protect them in their misfortune than to resist them while
they were in power (*Madame de Staël,* 212-213).

And he praises Julie Talma in similar terms:

She hated the party opposed to hers, but she devoted
herself with zeal and perseverance to the defense of any
individual whom she saw oppressed; [. . .] in the midst
of political tempests, during which everyone was at one
time or another the victim, we often saw her lending all
the support of her action and her courage to persecuted
people, on both sides at once (*Julie,* 187).

In Power, with the Opposition

If we take an overview of Constant's political en-
gagements, we can distinguish two kinds. Either he is
on the side of the power, as was the case briefly in 1795
when he collaborated with Louvet and in 1815 when he
helped Napoleon; or he places himself frankly among
the opposition, and benefits from his membership in a
deliberative body to supervise and criticize the power,
as in 1800-1801 with the Tribunat and after 1817 with
the Chamber of Deputies. One can guess that this second type of commitment sat better with him. There are
many reasons. First, not being a party man, Constant is
not put up as a Councillor under pressure from his
comrades-in-arms, but thanks to the choice of a prince;
however, this favor is badly received by the public and
damages the chance of success of distinctly political

plans. The *Acte Additionel* to the Constitution, which he wrote for Napoleon during the Hundred Days, is remarkable in many respects, but the conditions in which it was established did not make it very popular. Moreover, the kind of "centrism" professed by Constant is more valuable as a political philosophy than as political action. It makes it possible to fight the extremes, to escape sectarianism and to remain faithful to an ideal rather than to a party; it is less certain that it could be a suitable basis for an effective government since it pushes all the regime's malcontents to those same extremes and thereby precludes the possibility of a legitimate succession.

In his role as a member of the opposition, on the other hand, Constant and his "centrism" are perfectly in their place.

The abstract principles of *human rights* and *citizens' rights* are not, in themselves, rules for everyday policy; but remembering them is essential in order to maintain limits on power, which otherwise tends to expand. That does not mean that Constant chooses the ethics of conviction over the ethics of responsibility. For him, the distinction would be meaningless, for he always took care to hold himself responsible for his convictions, to take the world as it is into account when formulating his ideals. Simply, his membership in the opposition releases him from any obligation to conduct himself with reserve, and ensures him a greater freedom.

Journalist and Deputy

One can thus grant to Constant that he remained, in practice, faithful to his own theory. He tried to combine the freedom of the Moderns (the maintenance of a private sphere free of any intervention by power) with the freedom of the Ancients, actively participating in public life. This participation is best expressed in two specifically modern forms. One is the publication of his opinions. In the old republics, smaller in size, the citizens could meet together and discuss their destiny. In the large modern nations such a solution is not possible — but there is a substitute. Indeed, books and the press provide a means of filling this void — they inform governments of their subjects' state of mind and at the same time offer to the subjects a form of recourse against arbitrary exercise of power.

"Publicity is the tool of the oppressed against the oppressor" (*Sur la censure des journaux,* 1296). In a world where the individual is likely to have only a private space, publications (as the term itself indicates) ensure access to the public space. Printing is the essential tool of modern democracy; but, for this tool to be accessible to all requires a pluralist press and publications not controlled in advance. Then each individual has a good chance of finding a vehicle of expression. Constant was intensely active as a journalist between 1795 and 1802 and, again, from his return to France in 1814 until his death in 1830; he published numerous newspaper articles and pamphlets.

The second form of participation consists of becoming, oneself, a representative of the popular will, or a deputy. Constant was elected to the Chamber from 1819 to 1822 and from 1824 to 1830. Having become one of the principal spokesmen of the liberal opposition, he would give a great number of speeches whose topics ranged from freedom of the press to the fight against slavery and France's colonial policy. He took his responsibilities seriously; one day he wrote to his cousin:

> My mission is to make, if it can be made, a constitutional government win. As long as I am appointed, I can think neither of myself or of what you call glory. [. . .] A portion of the people has entrusted its interests to me, and I owe them the sacrifice of my successes and my life (to Rosalie Constant, November 7, 1820).

Constant is not a politician who also left us a reflective work exposing the lessons of his experience. He is a thinker, philosopher and writer who cannot remain indifferent to the fate of the city and who decides to accept his responsibilities. His engagement was crowned with success, even if, since that time, we have forgotten Constant's many merits. Modern democracy as we know it today is the direct heir of the ideal that he defended.

The
"Misery of the Human Heart"

While interest is a powerful factor in the public sphere, it is by no means the only driving force; aspiration to justice (to equality) must also be considered. But what about the sphere of intimacy? Constant distinguishes the two domains and suggests an answer to this question in a text that contrasts the public person to the private person:

> Magistrate, judge, public figure, his duty undoubtedly is justice; but the most precious part of his private existence, over which society should have no jurisdiction, is to surround himself with other beings, people dear to him, those who are his peers, distinct from all the beings of his species. When it comes to other people, it is enough for him never to harm them and sometimes to serve them; but to this preferred circle, to this circle of

> love, emotion, memories, belong his devotion, his con-
> stant preoccupation, and every form of partiality
> (*Godwin*, 565).

Justice must reign in the public sphere. But in the private world of interwoven affinities and antipathies — perfectly legitimate in their place — equality does not apply. Here, it is not justice that reigns at the top of the hierarchy, it is love. We thus enter a new sphere, after that of public life: intimate life.

Egoistic Love

According to the first description of what Constant himself calls, at the end of *Adolphe*, "the misery of the human heart" ("Réponse," 82), one could say that the experience of love may begin in various ways but it always ends in failure, if not catastrophe.

The first approach that Constant considers is familiar to us from his political writings: that is, once again, the approach that consists in simply serving one's own interests as much as possible. Love as a form of selfishness — such seems to be the version that Constant explores in one period of his life. Isn't passion "of all feelings, the most egoistic" (*Adolphe*, VI, 52)? It occupies a large place in the diary entitled *Amélie et Germaine*, dating from 1803 (in which we are dealing with a confession, rather than a doctrine). Here, Constant conceives the game of desire as having only one player: the subject himself. It is true that he is referring to marriage rather than to love. He must make a decision regarding Germaine (de Staël): could he escape her by marrying Amélie, a young woman from Geneva? It is worth mentioning that these marriage plans never take into account the future bride's intentions. As for the rest, the choice of the object is completely secondary. "I should be married. But to whom?" (January 6, 1803). Or: "I positively need a wife. I need it politically" (March 2, 1803). A wife, rather than Amélie in particular. Even if, in the final analysis, it is Amélie who was to be selected, the questions that Constant asks relate only to himself. "The great question relating to Amélie is whether I wish to live in Paris or not" (February 5, 1803); and when he imagines a marriage proposal, he begins as follows: "I must [. . .] set forth for you my situation and my character and my principles on marriage" (February 3, 1803). And what if Amélie had her own "principles"?

But Amélie does not exist as a subject, that is, as an autonomous being with a will of its own. The same draft marriage proposal immediately dissolves the specific case into general reflections on love, happiness and the couple. Amélie does not interest Constant in herself, but only insofar as she may resemble an ideal form made up by him. "I love you even more, as that which I believe you may become" (February 3, 1803). On the other hand, he is scandalized to discover that, similarly, Amélie does not perceive his own singularity. Is a desire for marriage all that she has in her heart? — perhaps forgetting that he has nothing more in his own heart.

The *other* is reduced, in this *Journal,* to a purely auxiliary function. And that is intentional. Here is the abstract portrait that Constant sketches of his preferred object in marriage.

> I need a being whom I can protect, whom I can hold in my arms, whom it would be easy to make happy, whose inoffensive existence yields effortlessly to mine. I need a wife, in a word, who is almost imperceptible, except for my domestic affections, and who is a soft, intimate and easy part of my life. But where can I find this woman? (January 6, 1803).

A woman-object, one should say: a woman who exists to the least extent possible and, especially, who does not exist in and of herself; a woman who is nothing more than a part of his own life. Here is the ideal. And instead of that, he has Germaine: "What a man-like temperament!" (January 9, 1803).

However, Amélie could well be this insignificant person, and that is one reason she interests Constant. She is sufficiently young, stupid, and poor that he may be sure of having his way with her. "I am so far superior to her that she can only be an amusement to me" (January 26, 1803). "She would be easy to manage" (January 23, 1803). Taken to the extreme, Amélie is barely human:

> If one treated her gently, she would be a faithful enough animal [. . .]. I would never allow her to influence my

> behavior, even in small things [. . .]. Isn't it a good thing
> that a woman is by her very nature destined to a subor-
> dinate role? (February 19, 1803).

A poor, stupid and, in addition, slightly ugly
woman: perfect! But this too has its drawbacks, and
Constant hesitates to take the matrimonial plunge.

The solitary subject seldom speaks the language of
interest so frankly; true, this is in a private diary. But
Constant believes himself right in doing so: he follows
here the widespread view according to which self-
interest is the truth behind human behavior, the subject
is self-sufficient and, if one cannot do without them
completely, others must be reduced to the state of non-
subjects. "My spirit is sufficient unto itself," he writes
(January 15, 1803), and his only concern, after the marriage plan, would be to escape from others. "We are
sufficient to ourselves" would be, for him, the "greatest
happiness on earth"; the gravest misfortune, on the
other hand, would be to take into account "other people's opinions" (February 3, 1803).

Such is the general tenor of this diary. General, but
not exclusive. In the middle of a sentence, Constant
shows another side of himself, which suddenly deprives all that came before of any force of conviction.
He has just assured himself once again that he will easily subjugate Amélie. Then he adds: "Have I ever
dominated anybody? Let us act in good faith and not
write for ourselves as we do for the public. With a
good mind for ideas, I have very little strength" (March

2, 1803). All his dreams of subservience suddenly appear to be the reverse of his own life: that of a submissive being. Was the portrait of the ideal future bride anything but a reversed image of Germaine, whom Constant had before his eyes every day? Perhaps that is a characteristic of Constant as an individual. But this sentence contains another revelation — that all of the above and all that follows is written "for the public." This reminder also applies to his wish. Locking yourself up at home with your spouse does not free you of dependence on others. The dream of egoistic interest is condemned to failure, for it does not correspond to the truth of the human heart; the egocentric explanation falls short. No more than it helps us understand all public conduct can interest — immediate or longer term — get beyond the surface of our experiences in love.

The Ideal of Fusion

Then a second attitude, seemingly much more generous, comes up: seeing the other person as one's equal and aspiring to fuse with her. That was Constant's attitude as a young person. In reconsidering his first marriage, and in imagining its development, he says with regret: "Neither one nor the other would any longer think of being just one — such a delicious dream," *Journal*, April 26, 1805). The characters of *Adolphe* also share this ideal. Adolphe seeks to charm Ellénore with statements faithful to the idea of fusion. He promises to be "concerned only with you, existing only for you" (III, 28). He perceives his own existence as "lost within yours" (III, 32). And that is indeed what he gets from Ellénore — she becomes "a being who was devoted so uniquely to me" (V, 43).

One can already see, however, that Constant has serious reservations about espousing this ideal. The dream of fusion may be delicious, but what good is it to delude oneself with pure dreams? Elsewhere in the *Journal*, Constant insists on the contrary: one individual never fuses with another. "The others are others, one can never make them oneself [. . .]. Between us and that which is not us stands an insurmountable barrier" (December 18, 1804).

If the love between two beings leads to the creation of a single being, it is because one of the two chose, or was constrained, to self-immolate in favor of the other. Fusion is, actually, hardly different from subservience. Ellénore's fate in *Adolphe* illustrates this after she accepts fusion not only in words, as Adolphe does, but also in her actions. She says it herself — "Love was my whole life; it could not have been yours" (X, 74-5). Her destiny illustrates this equation. Having lost love (having read Adolphe's letter to the Baron de T***), she does not hesitate to lose her life. "What is my crime?" she asks in her posthumous letter. "Loving you, being unable to exist without you?" (X, 79). Even if it is not a crime, this form of love ("being unable to exist without you") is indeed responsible for her misfortunes. The consequences of this love, seen as fusion, are disastrous. It is better, one might conclude, that apart from his passion in love, each being should have his own activity, a public career, which makes him autonomous — and therefore less vulnerable.

The Logic of Desire

Egoistic love is a mirage; so is the ideal of fusion. Where, then, is the truth of love? The third way explored by Constant, which occupies a greater place in his life and in his work, holds love to be a *lack*, and it is reduced thus to the logic of desire. The more general formulation of this law of Constant's seems to be: "My heart is tired of all that it has and laments all that it does not have" (*Journal*, September 16, 1812).

This law has foreseeable consequences, the first one being that the obstacle, or the perceived impossibility of fulfilling the desire, reinforces it and keeps it going. Constant's writings abound in scenes that illustrate this rule. Love lasts as long as "interest in the challenge persists" (*Mémoires de Juliette*, "Adrien de Montmorency," 302). All we have to do is to announce the end of a relationship, and we may find a taste for it again. In the presence of no matter how small an obstacle, love can be rekindled. "While believing you are separating me from her, you could well attach me to her forever," Adolphe writes to his father (V, 46). The

history of a desire, in its ascendant phase, is an enumeration of obstacles overcome. Thus, in chapters III
and IV of *Adolphe*, the stages are: 1. permission to see
Ellénore, after the declaration of love; 2. the right to
see her alone; 3. the possibility of speaking to her
about love; 4. obtaining a pledge of reciprocity; 5.
physical love.

The second application of the law is only the reciprocal of the first. In the absence of any obstacle, desire
dies. "Reassured as to Cécile's heart, I blush to acknowledge it, I put a lower value on that which I no
longer feared I might lose" (*Cécile*, II, 148). And Adolphe ends up hoping for his father's opposition to his
relationship with Ellénore, for otherwise this relation
becomes unbearable to him. Indeed, it is likely to en-
gage in the downward phase of desire: since it consisted of a lack, the lack of the lack kills it. Adolphe had
conquered Ellénore; henceforth, "she was no longer a
goal, she had become a bond" (IV, 34). He continues to
maintain a common life, "still finding pleasure there,
but no longer finding charm" (IV, 37). If the other does
not ask anything of me, I want to give her everything.
"I felt I had obligations precisely because she appeared
to believe I had none" (*Cécile*, VI, 162). If, on the contrary, the other gives me everything, I cannot desire her
anymore: "I was touched, but to despair, by the new
sacrifice that Ellénore made for me" (*Adolphe*, VI, 49).

Thus, loving somebody, falling in love, is hardly a
sentiment that leaves the subject's heart and gets fixed,

without an intermediary or specific event, on the selected object. The birth of love is described more or less identically in *Adolphe* and *Cécile*. Its first moment is the imitation of a third party — love comes from the outside, not the inside. In *Adolphe*, it is "a young man" who chooses Adolphe as a confidant of his adventures in love: "The spectacle of such happiness made me regret not having experienced it yet" (II, 18). In *Cécile*, paradoxically, it is his own wife whom the narrator envies in the same manner. She has an extraconjugal adventure that, instead of making him jealous, awakens in him the desire to imitate her.

> "I could not prevent myself from envying these two hearts intoxicated with love. [. . .] 'How happy they are!' I tell myself while returning to my room, 'and why should I be deprived of such happiness?'" (I, 138).

We begin by comparing ourselves to others, just as Rousseau melancholically describes the beginning of humanity in the *Discours sur l'origine de l'inégalité.* If the third party is decidedly not an example to imitate, then it is a danger to avoid. "If anything decides me in her favor [that of Amélie], it will be Germaine, Germaine who is increasingly more anxious, more irritable, more demanding" *(Amélie et Germaine,* February 1, 1803). "Mme. de Malbée's impetuosity pushed me toward the idea of marrying Cécile" *(Cécile,* V, 160).

Here is love ready to be born; now it needs an object. Its choice is always due to chance, to a pure conjunction of circumstances. In *Cécile,* it hinges on a turn of the conversation. "Upon hearing her name, I suddenly said to myself that perhaps she would fulfill my goal better than any of the women whose image I had sought to redefine" (I, 138). The image precedes its object. In *Adolphe,* it is on the strength of a fortuitous invitation that the choice of Ellénore occurs:

> Tormented by a vague emotion, I want to be loved, I told myself, and I looked around; I saw no one who inspired me to love, no one who appeared likely to accept it; I examined my heart and my tastes: I felt not the slightest sense of any preference (II, 19).

And, the introductions having been made:

> Offered to my view at a moment when my heart needed love, and my vanity needed success, Ellénore seemed to me to be a conquest worthy of me (II, 21).

Every time, it is public opinion or the word of some third party that determines the choice. This woman becomes desirable because a conversation presents her as such. She does not satisfy a requirement coming from the depth of one's soul, but the vanity of the hero, his pride — that is, the image he has made of the image that others have made of him.

The model to be followed is present; a fortuitous circumstance has made it possible to choose an object; but that is not quite enough. An obstacle must still crop up. The episodes in *Adolphe* and *Cécile* are parallel once again. In *Cécile* , the narrator sends a declaration of love in which he hardly believes:

> I was not at all in love with her, when I sent it to her; but upon her reply, which was proper, witty, cold, polite, and which ended in an absolute refusal to receive me in the future, I felt or believed myself to feel the most violent passion (I, 139).

The same situation applies in *Adolphe* :

> She answered me kindly, gave me affectionate advice, offered a sincere friendship to me, but told me that until the Count de P*** returned, she could not receive me. This answer upset me. My imagination, irritated by the obstacle, took over my whole existence (II, 23).

Such are the necessary and sufficient conditions for love: imitation, fortuitous circumstances, an obstacle. Nothing that comes from oneself, nor even from the other-object — only the principle of desire, sensitivity to the context, and sociability take care of everything. The other features of love referred to in *Adolphe* do not contradict this image. It is the impression (which we know to be illusory) of a loved being that was created exclusively for us, a passion that strikes us without any intervention of our will, the illusion of invulnerability, and the sharp divide between, on one side, exaltation and, on the other, "vulgar concerns" (IV, 33), or "that forgetting of all one's interests, of all one's duties" (VI, 50).

Such is the conceited, passive love-passion, deluded with dreams.

Submitted to its relentless logic, the human subject does not seem to have any chance of finding happiness in love. It cannot, however, be prevented from aspiring to it. "My aim in marrying is to find love, and much more to be loved by my wife than to love her," Constant states, a little bit haughtily (*Amélie et Germaine,* January 15, 1803), and his character says: "I want to be loved, I thought" (*Adolphe,* II, 19). But the truth is otherwise: being loved does not make one happy, and thus one should not wish for it. "Nobody was ever more loved, more praised, more cherished than I, and never was a man less happy," observes Constant (*Journal,* April 20, 1805). Or, in a letter to Rosalie, written one year before his death: "I wished for many things in my life; I obtained almost all of them and, after having obtained them, I lamented my success" (November 15, 1829). But how can one keep oneself from wishing to be loved?

So this is the everyday tragedy of desire. I love; but I only have a choice between two misfortunes. Either the object of my love responds to the call, and desire dies; or she does not do so, and desire is frustrated. In this, Constant sees fate, and he affirms that highlighting this was his intention in *Adolphe.* Would all of human life be reduced to such "a choice between two evils"? Constant sometimes gives the impression that he likes to discover this same fate expressed in other people's works: Corinne and Oswald, in Mme. de Staël's novel, "cannot be happy together, nor could they be happy anymore when apart" *(Madame de Staël,* 226). The sentences of *Adolphe* are not very different: "It is a dreadful misfortune not to be loved when one loves; but it is also terrible to be loved passionately when one no longer loves" (V, 43). Once relieved of the presence of Ellénore, he would not be any "less anxious, less agitated, less dissatisfied" ("Lettre à l'Editeur," 82).

And there we have the third and last type of love life, ending, in its turn, in one or the other form of misfortune.

Loving

How well does Constant's sentimental life illustrate the laws of desire that the writer proposes to his reader?

First, it must be said that Constant was perfectly familiar with the effects of his logic. The *mal du siècle* that struck him in his youth already modeled this two-sided dead-end. "I will pass like a shadow over the earth, drifting between misfortune and boredom," he wrote emphatically to Isabelle de Charrière (September 17, 1790). As soon as he is surrounded by those who love him, he is bored; as soon as he does not feel loved, he is unhappy. All his life is "an alternation between suffering and ennui" (to the countess of Nassau, August 2, 1808). Indeed, knowing this alternating dynamic by heart, he scolds himself bitterly:

> What an animal I am! Doubly animal! Both in my chimerical fears and in my feelings that are re-ignited by these fears, and which then subside too much when I am reassured (*Journal*, December 9, 1806).

Anna and Juliette

Two of Constant's adventures in love are good illustrations of the complementary roles in this logic of desire, the satiated pursued and the insatiable pursuer; in other words, with Anna Lindsay and Juliette Récamier.

Benjamin meets Anna in November 1800 and discovers with her the plenitude of sensual love. The language he speaks in his letters is that of fusion: I am you, you are within me, we are one being, let us live only one for each other. "You embody all that I value in life; each drop of my blood pulses only for you, alone!" (December 13, 1800). "I will devote all my life to you" (December 14, 1800). "Only you meet all the aspirations of my spirit, all the desires of my heart" (December 25, 1800). "All that is not you is foreign to me. The world is nothing to me any longer" (December 30, 1800).

Nearly two months go by in this euphoria. In mid-January 1801, Benjamin starts to sense how much hyperbole infused the preceding effusions. His life is not limited to love experiences; he also has political and literary ambitions. He aspires to power, fortune, glory —

but he pursues them, he now affirms, only for the purpose of being able to offer them to Anna. She, meanwhile, is no longer the only person that he knows: there is Germaine, whom he no longer loves, indeed, but with whom he does not wish to break off; and he himself is not the only person in Anna's life. She has children, and also a former protector and lover (like Ellénore in *Adolphe*, as has frequently been observed). Benjamin still loves her passionately; but he is no longer willing to ignore or disguise reality.

Anna, however, continues on the initial trajectory and, giving herself fully, still demands everything in return; for Benjamin, this all-consuming demand starts to become burdensome. So he begins to back off. No, he is not capable of making Anna completely happy; it would be better if each of them preserves some autonomy so that they can appreciate each other the more. He carefully chooses the expressions he employs in his letters. He no longer aspires to make her happy, only to not prevent her being happy. He will do anything for her, except that which could bring her harm — in other words, she should not break off with her former lover. But every time he retreats, Anna demands more. "I do not know by what spell my love is increased every day," she writes him now (April 14, 1801), perhaps unaware that the spell is woven by the very logic of desire. At the same time, she notes that their relationship has become asymmetrical. "He can live without me, and I die when we are far apart" (May 25, 1801). Anna gives him everything; because of that, Benjamin wants (practically) nothing. Two years later, this is how he would indicate the state of mind he already felt with her: "Fear of boredom is my dominant impulse" *(Amélie and Germaine,* January 6, 1803).

A (temporary) rift comes when Anna asks Benjamin for proof of his detachment from Germaine. He has to admit: even if they are no longer in love, he is not ready to terminate that relationship, or to give up his freedom:

> For me, while devoting to you a large part of my life because I find happiness with you, I want the independence which I have always preserved, I do not want to destroy any ties of friendship, of recognition and of affection, nor to be ungrateful nor perfidious nor to be submitted to any kind of yoke. [. . .] I want to sanction my feeling for you by the only thing that makes that feeling happy and durable — freedom (May 31, 1801).

Anna understands that this is by no means a plan for a life together, and she breaks up with him. Benjamin concludes in his *Journal,* three years later: "She is perhaps the woman who loved me the most, and she is one of those who made me the most unhappy" (July 28, 1804).

Juliette Récamier is a friend (perhaps also a lover) of Germaine de Staël; Benjamin has known her for a long time but, one day in August, 1814, the famous coquette dares him to try. Benjamin offers everything, right from the start. "Career, ambition, scholarship, spirit, entertainment, it has all disappeared. I am no longer anything but a poor being that loves you" (to Juliette Récamier, October 1, 1814). "I love only you, I live only for you [. . .], the rest is anguish and confusion" (November 1, 1814). "Obeying you is my goal, my only goal, as loving you is my only life" (January 27, 1815). Doesn't that sound like Ellénore, the heroine of *Adolphe,* whose lines Constant wrote six or seven years before?

All this could only annoy Juliette, who is a devote of the logic of desire. This man who sacrifices everything for her leaves her nothing more to wish for. She thus takes refuge in an indifference that need not be feigned, which further exacerbates Benjamin's desire. He no longer asks, he begs her to have pity on him: "If your door were closed to me, I would lie down in the street in front of your door" (January 23, 1815). He does not balk at blackmail: I am suffering, I am dying, I will commit suicide. "If it were not so cruel to commit suicide without anybody taking interest, I would not resist the desire that impels me" (November 6, 1815). But Juliette remains cold as marble.

Was Benjamin forgetting all his theoretical knowledge on the logic of desire, to act so pathetically? Not at all. In the midst of his supplications, he notes lucidly, "Because I love you, I have lost everything in your eyes" (March 7, 1815). He knows the rules of the game. "The less we do, the more she will do" (*Journal,* November 6, 1814). "To obtain something, let us not request anything" (November 21, 1814). He anticipates the result: "If she liked me, I would tire of this to some extent" (February 10, 1815). He knows from the beginning that Juliette is a flirt who is not interested in him; but knowing is one thing, acting is another. Desire does not obey one's will. Benjamin tries hard to apply his theories, but he cannot. He even thinks that there is a providential justice in that. Juliette is only an instrument in the invisible hand which leads him to discover the role complementary to that which he usually plays, to make him expiate the sufferings which he himself has inflicted (on Anna Lindsay, for example, whom he is seeing again at the same time). "I suffered because I made others suffer, and precisely as I had made them suffer" (to Juliette, September 9, 1815).

For, reduced to the role of a frustrated agent of desire, Benjamin suffers while Juliette is annoyed. "I fight against an appalling pain. [. . .] An extraordinary pain that never lets up" (*Journal*, October 3-4, 1814). "Fever, anguish. [...] Devastating sadness, agitated night" (February 15, 1815). "I fell into all my old most frantic despondency. [. . .] Dejection and dreadful pain. Terrible night" (September 2-3, 1815). "Returned home in despair. What a dreadful yoke, and I cannot break it" (October 8, 1815). He is always reduced to choosing between two evils: "My God, when someone is suffering for you, how painful life is, and when one suffers no more, how insipid life is!" (to Juliette, June 5, 1816). However, all in all, Benjamin prefers his present role.

Long afterwards, he refers to it with a certain nostalgia — "the memory of the most painful, but most animated, days of my life" (February 16, 1823). Why? Because to suffer is, despite everything, to live; to experience nothing is to die. "To love is to suffer — but it is also to live — and I had not been alive for so long!" (September 2, 1814). At the end of October 1815, Benjamin manages nevertheless to tear himself away from his anguish by leaving Paris.

Anna and Juliette are not only the examples of this type of behavior on Constant's part. With regard to his wife, Charlotte, he writes one day in his *Journal*:

> I will do my best to arrange it so that I give the impression of wanting to subject her to my plans, so that she will feel she has won in reclaiming her liberty; whereas, if I offered it to her, she would instead wish to take my liberty (October 11, 1812).

The ways of desire can be quite tortuous.

A Wound That Can Never Be Healed

Certain 19th century commentators, in particular Sainte-Beuve, when reading some of these texts (and others, like that cited above from *Amélie et Gemaine),* thought they were in a position to make a peremptory assessment of Constant as a man in his relations with women. They took the texts as proof that he was unable to love, that his heart was sterile, that he was a cold calculator; as though "the misery of the human heart" were only that of the individual, Benjamin Constant. These charges would not deserve mention were it not for the frequency with which they have been repeated. Without going into the reasons that could motivate Constant's detractors (Pierre Déguise has done this well), we should note first off that there is a great difference between the egoistic and calculated act, assuming it is proven as such, and the description of this act, produced by its author. The word is never transparent; the statement does not flow automatically from the action. Should we chastise Constant for such egoistic thought when his personal writings testify above all to his implacable lucidity, not to say his cruelty to himself? Moreover, as will soon be seen, the games of desire described here by Constant are far from the only form of love that is accessible to him. But even more important: it is not clear that these descriptions are to be taken literally. It is worth asking whether their function is simply to state the truth, or rather to dissimulate a confession that is more difficult to make?

Constant's appreciation for the personage of Julliette Récamier can help us to refine our understanding of this. Juliette is a pure incarnation of the logic of desire that he himself seemed to consider as true and that he believed he was observing at work in his own life. However, when he analyzes Juliette's behavior, he proposes another interpretation. Her coquetry, the art of eliciting desire without giving anything, is only a facade for her "incapacity of feeling," made up of "indifference and of barrenness, not only for me but for everyone" (*Journal*, September 24, 1815). Juliette claims to dominate love; in reality, she is frightened by it. It is a handicap that she passes off as a form of control. "When devotion is presented to her, in any form she might prescribe, she is afraid of it and torments it without wanting it. She could transform love into heaven on earth; but she refuses to do so." Incapable of experiencing love in its presence, Juliette dedicated herself to worshiping it in its absence. But this worship does not tell the truth about love, it only masks regret. And Juliette bears all the consequences: "She is not happy and she does not give happiness" (*Mémoires de Juliette,* "Lucien Buonaparte," 293), for in human relations a very different law applies: "We receive only that which we give" (to Juliette, December 7, 1815).

However, there is more than one resemblance between Juliette and Benjamin himself, and he does not fail to notice that. His first great friend, the Scotsman John Wilde, characterized him thus at the age of eighteen: "A slave to the passion of love, which, however, is constantly changing its object" (J. Wilde, 372). Thirty years later Constant writes in connection with Juliette: "She did not love the weeping man in love, but she loved the love that made him weep" (*Mémoires de Juliette,* "Lucien Buonaparte," 290). To love love rather than its object: isn't this the very definition of love as something missing, of the desire for something that is wanting, the logic of which is laid out in the length and breadth of Constant's writings? But if he is so able to see other people's limitations and delusions, shouldn't we turn his perspicacity toward himself and ask a few questions as to what is hiding behind these allegations of his?

One would have all the more grounds for doubting the universal validity of the theories of the desire-as-lack if one bore in mind that they relate only to one of the varieties of love experiences of Constant himself: those that concern his relations with Anna and Juliette, specifically, and, before, with Mme. Trevor and Mlle. Pourrat, or with his first wife, Minna. But the attraction that he feels for Isabelle de Charrière, first, and for Germaine de Staël later, is of a very different character. They are strong, intellectual women and artists, and the harmony of the spirits counts more than the physical conquest. Although he no longer lives with Germaine, he can write to his friend Prosper de Barante: "As long as this other person is alive, I will not be alone. My mind is connected to hers. My pages are letters that I write to her" (September 23, 1812). Lastly, the women who make him particularly happy are different still. These are Mme. de Johannot and his second wife Char-lotte, the maternal women who love him as he is, for what he is, and no matter what he does; they do not ask anything of him in return, and suddenly he is ready to be very generous with them.

We should digress here and look at the biography

not as a form of expression on the part of its author, but as an incentive to pursue the interpretation of his texts. It is known that Constant's life began with a trauma: his mother's death in childbirth. That was also Rousseau's fate but, in his case, the shock was attenuated by the presence of an affectionate father and people who cared for the child in a relatively stable manner. Not so for Constant. His father, a career military officer, lived elsewhere, and returned to his son only to tear him out of one relationship and to thrust him into a different one; to inflict a certain tutor on him, shortly to be replaced by some other, then another still. He finally entrusted Benjamin to a governess who was actually his own mistress, and who would become the mother of his other children.

This is the disastrous emotional context in which the young Benjamin grew up. Whether or not this was the cause of some of his later choices, one thing is certain. Constant has the greatest difficulty in accepting his love affairs in their presence. His life unfolds in such a way that, with regard to the women he meets, he is torn between two contrary attitudes: on the one hand, to ask them to fill the gaping hole left open by the untimely disappearance of his mother, but at the same time, to punish them in retaliation with the abandonment of which he was victim. Women must love him so he can leave them and show everyone (and thus himself) that he has no need of them. The need is twofold, and he can only be unhappy for he can never satisfy it entirely.

If this assumption is right, all the verbiage about love as a lack would be only the disguise of an even more painful admission — recognition of the ineffaceable trauma left by the mother's disappearance, thus the acceptance of the child in him, vulnerable and dependent.

Not having been the object of a continuous and unquestionable love during the decisive years of early childhood, Constant does not trust himself, does not love himself, is not persuaded of the need for his existence or of his real value. This may be the root of his acute feeling of nothingness, his doubting of his own existence. "I am not entirely a real being" (*Journal*, April 11, 1804). "Sometimes I touch myself to find out whether I am still alive. I seem to live out of courtesy, the way I tip my hat in the street at people who greet me and whom I do not know" (to Prosper de Barante, September 23, 1812). From this stems his constant toying with the idea of death (his duels are as numerous as his suicide attempts). As he writes to his aunt, "I have this specific problem that the idea of death never leaves me. It weighs upon my life, it corrodes all my plans [. . .] — it is not the fear of death, but a detachment from life" (to the countess of Nassau, February 1, 1805). This is also the source of his excessive need for external recognition, whether it comes from a person or from a community, a relationship with a person, or collective action, an affair or a political career. Recognition serves to confirm his existence and reassures him of his merits. He says in a letter to Claude Hochet:

It is a great misfortune not to love oneself enough, not to take a serious enough interest in oneself. [. . .] The thing I am interested in must be outside of myself. Otherwise, I immediately make a deal with myself, agreeing that the good I am doing myself is not worth the trouble I cause myself (June 12, 1812).

Even so, even this thing or this person outside himself cannot make him happy.

Let us juxtapose with these analyses a page from the diary that reveals a distress even deeper than those of which Constant usually complains. Isn't this what makes him say, when speaking about his life: "Nobody suspects which form of madness overwhelms him and lays him waste"? (March 13, 1805).

Friend and Father

Usually, friendship and parental love, more than sexual love, allow one to learn to cherish the presence of others. Constant has left no extensive reflections on the topic of friendship, even if he speaks of it in eulogistic terms in his letters to Prosper de Barante who was, between 1805 and 1815, his closest friend. Perhaps his frequent changes of residence during the first fifty years of his life explain the scarcity of his long-term friendships. (Although they do bequeath to us, on the other hand, an abundant correspondence. "A letter is a true happiness," writes Constant to Barante, October 11, 1811). Two of his best friends are women, Isabelle de

Charrière and Julie Talma; they die one after the other in 1805, when he is not yet forty years old. His closest confidante is his cousin Rosalie. He carries on a correspondence with her throughout his life. He explained it once: "You are my sister, by heart and by adoption. Fate felt it owed me this compensation after the trick nature played on me" (to Rosalie, March 15, 1811). Would Constant be willing to admit the decisive role his mother's death played in his life? He seems to do so, also in this page of the *Journal*:

> A feeling that life has given me, and that does not leave me, is a kind of terror of Destiny. I never draw a line to cross off a day, and I never write the date of the next day, without a feeling of concern as to what the unknown day might bring (January 19, 1805).

Catastrophe stalks him at every step.

With his father, relations are always difficult. Constant also has, with Germaine de Staël, a daughter, Albertine; but uncertainties in his relationship with the mother mean that he is not able officially to assume the position of father. His affection for Albertine, however, never dims. (This is rare enough to deserve mention: Montaigne, we know, is not interested in his children and does not even remember how many of them died at an early age; La Rochefoucauld is bitterly disappointed by his son; Rousseau gives up his children; and the list could go on). Every mention of Albertine in the diary is positive. Constant boasts that she resembles him; he admires her words and gestures, trembles when she is ill, and aspires to marry Germaine in order, among other things, to be able openly to play the role of father. After the break with Germaine, which also means the abandonment of Albertine, references to her become more melancholic: "Albertine's birthday. Alas! Alas!" (May 8, 1813). "Albertine is charming, clever as can be, adorable. It is she whom I miss. I would like to spend my life with her" (May 13, 1814). But Albertine grows up, marries, and this dream will never be fulfilled, of course. He writes nevertheless to Prosper de Barante: "Among the opportunities life offers, the relationship of a father and daughter is perhaps one of those that offer the most happiness" (April 7, 1813).

Constant seems to know that to love someone is, as he writes in *Adolphe*, "to revel in her presence" (III, 27) and he aspires to this state from his youth onward. ("The intimacy of the present moment is all that I desire," he writes to Isabelle de Charrière, July 27, 1787). Circumstances do not permit him to enjoy this experience. However, a change occurs around his fiftieth year. At the end of 1816, he settles for good in Paris, moving in with his second wife, Charlotte, who will be his most stable and happiest emotional relationship. He also conducts a dedicated public life as a writer and politician. It is not ecstasy but, compared to the preceding years, the last years of Constant's life are a time of serenity. He stops keeping his personal diary, his private life posing no more problem to him, and he is no longer worried by the miseries of the human heart. To what can we attribute this change? The cruel mirror that his relationship with Juliette held up to him might have some bearing on this, and the publication of *Adolphe* in 1816 as well, a publication preceded by many readings in private salons, in the course of which apparently both reader and listeners shed copious tears. Constant is not Adolphe, of course, but he gave this character one of the personalities that lived in him; and, consequently, exorcised it.

"The misery of the human heart" has more to do with Adolphe than Constant. One has difficulty in believing that Adolphe could have written this novel.

"A Two-Sided
and Enigmatic Being"

We can see now that Constant's thoughts on intimate life are not limited to the well-known theories of egoistic interest, fusion as an ideal, or desire defined as lack — theories that are quite old and are certainly present in his texts (as they are, since his time, among various thinkers of the 20th century), but which are used, in his case, to prohibit access to a dangerous area rather than to describe the world impartially. While using the language and the arguments of these theories, Constant gives us his own social thought, which is not reduced to these theories alone.

I, You, They

The subject does not exist alone in the world; he is necessarily constituted in relation to one or more individual *you*'s and impersonal *they*'s. There is something excessive and odd in Adolphe, who comments while observing himself: "I was not moved by any impulse emanating from the heart" (V, 40). We know that even Constant, exceptionally easy to influence, is not as non-existent as Adolphe. But in this extreme form an assertion is expressed whose scope is more general, namely that relationships, affections, loves constitute the very fabric of human existence. There is no *I* without *you*. Affection is "all there is in life" (*Journal*, August 1, 1807). "I have life and reality only in affection," Constant writes in a letter to Juliette Récamier (January 24, 1815), and in another: "What is life when one cannot be loved anymore?" (October 8, 1815). In a document dating from the beginnings of his relation with Germaine de Staël, he already spoke of her as of a person "without whom there is no more interest for me, no emotion on this earth" (Jasinski, 27). Integral selfishness is impossible, rather than immoral. This truth is too often ignored by those, such as Malthus, who build theories based on the idea that man remains exclusively concerned with his own personal interest:

> Man is not just an arithmetical symbol, there is blood in his veins and a need for attachment in his heart. [. . .] Everyone knows how the blind man answered when he was reproached for feeding his dog. "And who will love me then?" he said. (*Filangieri*, II, 5, 271)

Isn't this small anecdote, which everyone immediately recognizes as true, more telling than volumes of reasoning on the rational needs of man? It follows, as Constant wrote to Juliette Récamier, that one receives only that which one has given, and that the more one gives, the richer he is. Emotional wealth consists of the intensity of the relationships; to love more passionately is to live more intensely.

That is not the whole lesson that Constant derives from his "observation of the human heart." We should add, there is no *you* or *I* without *they* — third parties, public opinion. Rousseau, certainly, had discovered that humanity begins the moment we become conscious of being observed by a third party, but he bitterly laments this fall of "natural man" (who was thus not completely a man). Constant, too, aspired in his youth to release himself from this need to be recognized by other people's regard, and he boasts about it in his letters to Isabelle de Charrière. Her reply is stinging. "You say that you scorn public opinion because you see it heading in other directions. [. . .] *Because* does not apply; you do not scorn, you could never scorn, public opinion" (May 13, 1792).

Constant takes this lesson to heart and assumes without any shame what the earlier moralists might condemn under the name of "vanity." Being human, we need to be noticed by others — it is useless to revolt against what makes up our very identity. This dependence on others is even stronger than self-interest, and it wins out if the two come into conflict. "We exaggerate the influence of personal interest. Personal interest requires the existence of other people before it can act" (*Conquête*, II, 13, 194). "For everyone, opinions and vanity are stronger than interests " (*Polythéisme*, II, XI, 3, 63). Man "aspires, in his thought as in his behavior, to be approved by others, and external approbation is necessary for him to be satisfied internally" (II, XIII, 1, 130). Liaisons with others, as we also learned in *Adolphe*, end up becoming "so intimate a part of our existence" (V, 43). The separation between what is outside of us and what is inside is quite relative, since no *I* can exist without *you* and *they*.

All of Constant's accounts contain examples of this dependence on other people's view. In *Ma Vie*, he remembers one of his first adventures — his aim was not to become a woman's lover, but to make people around him believe that he had done so:

> The pleasure of making others say, and of hearing them say, that I keep a mistress consoled me, while in fact I was spending my life with a person whom I did not love at all, and keeping a mistress whom I paid but did not possess (91) .

If the narrator wants to possess Cécile, it is only out of "conceit," following a conversation between men (*Cécile*, VI, 161). Adolphe, in corresponding circumstances, is in turn driven by "a theory of self-conceit" (III, 30), and he describes his own desire for Ellénore as a satisfaction derived from attracting glances from third parties:

> If Heaven had granted me a woman whom social con-

ventions enabled me to acknowledge, whom my father did not blush to accept as his daughter, I should have been exceedingly happy to make her happy (VII, 58).

The father's and society's considerations override Adolphe's and Ellénore's desires.

These examples of "vanity" or, in more neutral terms, of inevitable dependence on the gazes and the words of others, are only one conspicuous illustration of what constitutes the substance of any human existence: sociability. Often, in fact, features of character or well-internalized state of minds prove to have the same origin. Thus the father's timidity in *Adolphe,* causing an "internal suffering [. . .], that chokes back in our hearts the deepest feelings, that freezes our words, that curdles in our mouth everything that we try to say" (I, 14); but what is timidity if not internalized fear of other people's judgement? And so, too, the shame that seizes the narrator and that is present, as a silent spectator, at his meeting with Cécile. "A repentance, a shame that pursued me even in the midst of pleasure" (VI, 162). *Cécile* contains another revealing scene — the two lovers go to a masked ball, where they intensely enjoy the pleasure of being together in public without being recognized by the others. The charm is such that they decide to repeat it the following week; but impunity is no longer a surprise, and they do not enjoy it. "The crowd became tiresome to us, since we did not fear it any more" (VI, 167). Isn't this another proof that other people's gaze shapes our experiences?

The Desire for Independence

Thus one should not take literally the statements that strew Constant's literary and intimate writings, that repeatedly pine for complete "independence." The "liberty" of the individual in relation to his affections cannot be understood according to the model of the liberty of the citizen in relation to the State. Emotional independence is not equivalent to political autonomy. Independence is only one moment in the game of desire/lack, that moment when the subject has nothing more to wish for and seeks to escape boredom. The aspiration to solitude is a motif that may be heard again and again in Constant's *Journal* and his correspondence — but it is a desire that can never be fulfilled and which hides within itself another desire. Once separated from his first wife, Constant writes to Isabelle de Charrière:

> For more than a year, I have wished for this moment, I have been pining for complete independence; it has come and now I tremble! I am somehow dismayed at the loneliness that surrounds me, I am frightened to have nothing to care about, me who groaned so much at having to care about something (March 31, 1793).

Twenty years later, he notes in his *Journal*: "I so much wished to live alone, and today I quake at the thought of it" (October 27, 1814). Constant's calls for independence should not be read out of independently of what surrounds them.

Such is also the lesson of *Adolphe*. The hero believes himself to have a similar "burning desire for independence" (I, 14), at the beginning of his tale, and later he misses his old life of independence. But these claims are not to be taken literally, unless one is satisfied with the psychology proclaimed by Adolphe's father: "With your spirit of independence, " he writes a little naively to his son, "you always do what you do not want to do" (VII, 54). It is Adolphe himself who will discover the bitter truth at the end of his story. "Liberty" and "independence" were only relative values — relative to Ellénore and his relationship with her; once those are finished, the values represent nothing more for him; or rather, they show him their reverse: independence is the "desert of the world," freedom, "isolation" and the absence of love (X, 76).

> How much it weighed upon me, this freedom which I had missed so dearly! How much it used to hurt my heart, this dependence that had so often revolted me! [. . .] I was free indeed, I was no longer loved: I was alien to everyone (X, 79).

"Liberty" in relation to other people cannot be an ultimate goal; it is rather the mask that cloaks our wish to replace an unsatisfactory relationship with another one, more intense; it is the alibi one gives for wishing to turn away from the object that pursues him. An entirely independent life would be a meaningless life, and would endanger the very existence of its subject.

Neither should one mistake the meaning of another assertion which often comes up in Constant's works, namely that the aim of society is to support the individual, that the individual comes first. Personal freedom, Constant wrote for example in *Les Mémoires sur les Cent-Jours*, is "the principal goal, or more precisely, the only goal of human associations, the purpose for which governments exist" (II, 2, 212). Does Constant envisage society on the model of a private club which one joins in order to enjoy the conveniences? No; what he points out is that, in theory, it is government that must be in the service of the people and not the reverse.

As for man's sociability, Constant is categorical on the subject — there does not exist, and has never existed, an asocial man. He even reproaches the previous centuries' philosophers for this — to have imagined an ancestor of man — "natural man" — wandering about, alone in the forest. "If such were the natural state of man, how would man have gotten away from it?" To answer this question, the philosophers are obliged to imagine men deciding to live in society — a decision that already presupposes society, debate, the capacity to argue.

> Society, in this system, would be the result of the development of intelligence, while the development of intelligence is itself only the result of society (*Religion*, I, I, 8, 154).

This is why Constant explicitly gives up on returning to a human state anterior to society. "We began by supposing that man had existed without society, language, religion." However "society, language, and religion are inherent to man" (I, I, 1, 23). There is no need to look for a reason for sociability other than "man's nature." Apostrophizing Rousseau (without naming him), Constant continues: man "is not sociable because he is weak; he is sociable because sociability is in his essence" (24). And, "man is sociable because he is man, as the wolf is unsociable because he is *wolf*" (*Filangieri*, I, 8, 213: of course, this is a reference to the wolf of fables, not forests). Constant the "individualist" does not ask that "each individual be his own center" (*Religion*, I, "Préface ", XXXVII). Such a formula would be both false (for there is continuity between what is internal and what is external) and dangerous (for the isolated individual is particularly fragile).

"An Unknown Center "

But if the center of each individual is not within himself, where is it? The center shifts, Constant would answer. Sometimes it is located inside, sometimes outside of us. Essentially, no man is limited categorically to the here-and-now, to his biological needs and instincts.

> Man was always been haunted by the thought that he is not down here simply to enjoy, and that coming to life, propagating, and returning to dust might not make up his sole destiny (I, II, 2, 257-258).

The being that manages to satisfy all his needs is still not fulfilled; he is called by something that is outside of him.

> There exists in us a tendency that is in contradiction with our apparent higher goal and with all the faculties that help us toward this goal. These faculties, all adapted to our use, work together to serve us, they work toward our greater good, and accept us as a single center. On the contrary, the tendency which we have just described prompts us out of ourselves, urges us towards things that do not have our utility as their goal, and seems to take us towards an unknown, invisible center with no analogy to ordinary life and daily concerns. (I, I, 1, 31-32).

The egocentrism of the current action is opposed by that which one could call the allocentrism of these rarer but by no means exceptional gestures. Each is as natural as the other. "Nature, which gave man love of himself for his personal safeguarding, also gave him sympathy, generosity, and pity, so that he would not eliminate his fellow men" (*Filangieri*, IV, 6, 401) One might try to grasp the contents of this "mysterious provision" by observing the example that Constant gives (this list appeared in the 1806 *Principes de politique*, but would be supplemented and clarified in 1824 in *La Religion*). "All these passions have [. . .] something mysterious about them, something contradictory, " Constant writes.

> Love, that exclusive preference for an object that we
> could have passed up long ago, and that resembles so
> many others; the need for glory, the thirst for celebrity
> that should continue after we are gone; the pleasure we
> find in devotion, a pleasure contrary to our instinctive
> nature; the melancholy, the sadness without cause,
> within which is a pleasure that defies analysis (*Religion*,
> I, I, 1, 32-33).

Add to that a certain ecstasy before the immensity
of nature, that seizes us "in the silence of the night, at
the shores of the sea, in the solitude of the countryside,"
as well as "tenderness and passion" (30). It is within
this ecstasy that Constant situates the religious sentiment, the object of his research in this book. He defines
it as a response to our "being drawn toward the unknown, toward the infinite" (35), as "the need man feels
to communicate with the surrounding nature, and the
unknown forces which seem to animate this nature" (I,
II, 1, 219). Human sociability and religious feeling thus
form part of this more general allocentric "disposition."

What all these examples have in common is, first of
all, the apparent irrationality of our gestures, the absence of any immediate utility (they have nothing to do
with the logic of interest). More positively, they are
also characterized (except for melancholy, which is particularly enigmatic) by their allocentrism: nature and
God, the beloved being and that to which one devotes
oneself, the great ideals as the sources of glory have in
common the fact that they are located outside of the
subject, that they transcend him instead of remaining

immanent. There is no human being, thinks Constant, who does not experience this exaltation of transcendence. "The need for enthusiasm is constant" (V, XV, 1, 170). Finally, a functional characteristic: whereas all our other gestures and actions may serve but would not in themselves constitute ultimate goals, these "passions" can define the objective and therefore also the direction an existence takes; they are no longer a means but an end (I, I, 1, 30).

One should not be deluded by reassuring fantasies. Men are not driven by this need for transcendence *instead of* by their interests, they are driven by both. And that is why man is "a two-sided and enigmatic being," and why he finds himself "sometimes out of place on this earth" (34). In any situation, therefore, "the principal question is whether feeling [of enthusiasm, of transcendence, we might add] or interest prevails" (I, II, 2, 264). One might suggest that besides these two great motivators of human action there is a third, which is reason, reflection, intelligence. Aren't some of our actions the pure products of the latter? No, replies Constant, for reason is pliable and can serve any master; it is an instrument, not a force. "Logic can come up with insoluble syllogisms both for and against any proposition" (I, I, 3, 75). Reason does not deserve any specific prestige: whatever the objective to be attained, it can supply suitable arguments. The mind is "the vilest of instruments when it is separated from the conscience" (I, I, 4, 91). "In the name of infallible reason,

Christians were fed to the beasts, and Jews were sent to the butchers" (I, I, 3, 76). There are only two "systems," Constant concludes:

> One gives us interest as a guide, and wellbeing for our goal. The other offers us self-improvement as a goal, and as a guide, intimate feeling, self-abnegation and the faculty of sacrifice ("Préface," XXXIX).

What is the balance of power between these two facets of the human being? Here, too, we should not be soothed by illusions. Most of the time, it is interest that wins; the feeling of transcendence reigns only "in those hours so short and so dissimilar to all the rest of our existence" (I, I, 1, 31). Love itself, which at least everyone recognizes, holds in check the tendency to "make each one his own center and his own goal," manages only a "temporary inversion" (IV, X, 10, 190-191). Most men stifle this feeling: such is the pessimistic conclusion to which Constant "arrives at the age of sixty." "Men seem to be divided by nature into two classes: those whose intelligence rises above their interests and their personal relationships, and those who are limited to that sphere" (*Souvenirs historiques,* 80). The latter form the great majority of humanity. It doesn't matter much; what is essential is not what proportion of the population is animated by an ideal of justice and love, but that this ideal is inextinguishable:

> There will always be men for whom justice is a passion

and the defense of the weak is a need. Nature wanted this succession; no one ever could stop it, no one ever will stop it (*Conquête*, II, 18, 221).

In his analysis of politics, Constant managed to avoid two shoals by refusing subservience to tradition and, at the same time, to the supposed laws of our nature — that is, to the material interest — in order to affirm the liberty (in both senses of the word) of the individual. His analysis of the passions that rule over our intimate life follows a parallel line of thought. On the one hand, he recognizes that the individual regulates his own love affairs, instead of obeying the injunctions of family or society. In addition, while knowing and analyzing the forces of egoism and the impersonal laws of desire, he shows them to be insufficient to explain the need that one feels to love and to be loved, to transcend oneself to celebrate others. Believing oneself to be the center of the world is the modern disease that corrodes the public world as well as private life. This belief is reprehensible, not for moral reasons alone (that would hardly be reason enough to cast it aside), it is — fortunately — an illusion, a faulty interpretation of the world. Modern man is not condemned to pay the high price of his freedom, he is not obliged to choose between the traditional community and egoistic loneliness. He *can* do so, certainly, but he remains fully responsible for this choice.

The Anatomy
of Human Exchanges

"The Reciprocal Situation"

Let us return to that sociability — which, grounded in the need for transcendence, is at the same time one of its principal manifestations — and observe the concrete consequences of the individual's constant immersion in the network of human interactions. Here, there are no isolated entities but only relationships. Even the contrast between essence and accident does not carry sway in the world of inter-subjectivity. I do not love this being or this class of beings in itself — for they do not exactly exist in themselves — but the being that is in a certain position compared to me. In intimate life, the being in and of itself does not exist. Constant gave a general formulation of this law in his *Journal*: "The object that eludes your pursuit is necessarily very different from the one which pursues you" (May 2, 1804), and: "Everything depends on the reciprocal situation in

153

life" (April 26, 1805).

Many examples illustrate how the circumstances relate to the nature of the experience. In fact, we should go farther. What others call circumstances are, in reality, constitutive elements of the event. Thus in *Cécile* we see that the narrator is sincerely overwhelmed by Mme. de Malbée's reproaches until the moment he learns that she had addressed exactly the same reproaches to a rival; at once, the remarks lose their potency (VI, 169). Or at another moment, the narrator's servant sarcastically approves his abandoning of Mme. de Malbée; suddenly, this abandonment appears to the narrator to be a grave error. And in *Adolphe*, what decides the hero's feelings towards Ellénore?

> Ellénore's ties with the Count de P***, the disparity of our ages, the difference in our situations, my departure, which various circumstances had already delayed but whose time was approaching (IV, 35).

An understanding between the two is not impossible, in principle, but it would have to coincide with a "conducive moment" (VI, 52). As Adolphe says, when referring to the beginning of the relationship, "a seemingly very frivolous circumstance produced a major revolution in my disposition" (II, 18). Major revolutions depend on circumstances *seemingly* very frivolous — actually there is nothing frivolous for the circumstances constitute the essence. Everything depends on "the reciprocal situation." In the preface to the third

edition of *Adolphe,* Constant, who displays a certain indifference towards his book ("I do not attach any value
to this novel," 10), also affirms that it was born of a certain type of challenge:

> ... to convince two or three friends, come together in the
> countryside, of the possibility of making a novel inter-
> esting when its characters would be reduced to two,
> and their situation would be always the same (9).

Nothing in the documents contemporary with the
creation of the novel confirms this statement, which
seems a little like posturing. Could *Adolphe* have been
born from a purely formal plan? But one can also see in
this a precise allusion to Constant's psychological discovery. It is not the great adventures, not the sudden
changes of fortune that form the substance of our existence, but the microscopic inflections, gradations of position, the fact that a thought is silent once, said aloud
the next time. In *Adolphe*, "nothing happens" — a man
and a woman meet, then separate. But Constant has
discovered the intriguing interest induced by a sublimi-
nal plot, the reverberations that human beings generate
and pick up in one another. "I left, with those words;
but who can explain to me how it can be, that the feeling that dictated them to me was extinguished even before I had finished pronouncing them?" (VII, 56). Here
is the kind of event that Constant chooses to tell in *Adolphe.* The great effects all have small causes.

Constant calls this feature of the psychic life

"mobility." It is nothing more than a sensitivity to context and, consequently, an authenticity; but seen from outside it appears to be inconstancy and fickleness (here we find the cause of the reproaches addressed to Constant). This is what gives him the *raison d'être* for his diary: writing it down makes it possible to pin down the confusion, to circumscribe fluidity. "This Diary is a kind of history, and I need my own history as much as any other, in order never to forget or ignore myself" (December 21, 1804). In that, Constant eloquently continues the tradition of Montaigne.

This same mobility and instability that characterize the behavior of the individual extends to his interior (there is no rupture between outside and inside, as we have seen). Each human being is not only double, ego- and allocentric, it is multiple, for it is made up of his relations with others, and these others are legion and occupy a variety of positions compared to him. There are the others who make him passionate or tired, serene or anxious. There are also those who, although in different ways, provoke in each of us the schism between the being who acts and the one who is satisfied to observe the former, or that between oneself and the image which one has of this self. ("Practically everyone believes himself to be worse, or more irresponsible, than he is," *Adolphe*, "Préface" to the second edition, 7), or even that between the heart and vanity ("This vanity stands between Ellénore and me," II, 22) ,between the desired appearance and the experience lived ("all the more violent since I felt weaker," IX, 70). That one may be physically alone does not change anything in this matter — the others are always already within us. "One could say of the majority of men — when they are alone, they are still constrained and factitious" (*Journal*, December 1, 1804).

These multiple characters who live within us can never come to a perfect agreement; this is why the unity of the individual is an illusion. "There is no complete unity in man, and almost no one is ever entirely sincere nor entirely insincere" (*Adolphe*, II, 23). Sincerity is impossible because the human being is never perfectly homogeneous. "All my feelings are true, but they are such that they collide with each other," (*Journal*, February 20, 1805).

A Theory of Language

This reflection on inter-subjectivity leads to what one could call a theory on language, though Constant never gives it a systematic form. One can gather from it, first of all, that speech takes on simultaneously two quite distinct duties, that of referring to the world, and therefore providing information relating to it (which may be true or false); and that of having two or more individuals communicate, producing a certain effect on them, measurable in terms of good and evil. Adolphe is interested only in this second, communicative function. "I no longer considered my words in terms of the meaning they should contain but according to the effect that they would produce" (V, 44). This description obviously would not be applied to Constant's public speaking, his writings on politics and religion; but, with regard to intimate life, oral exchange or correspondence, he seems to conform to it. "I have nothing to say that you do not already know, I admit," he writes for example to Juliette Récamier, "but repeating it to you is a continual need" (January 23, 1815).

By observing the practice of communication, Constant discovers two great laws that govern it. The first relates to the effect words have on the person speaking, when the object of the speech is his own feelings; it is the consequence of our constant interdependence and of our mobility. One could call it the *law of treason* (this, too, conforms to Montaigne's teaching). Indeed, to indicate one's own feelings, to translate his reactions into words, is to change them. To describe a state of the heart that one has experienced is to describe it falsely for, after the description, it will no longer be what it was before. That is what Adolphe is constantly observing. "As long as I was speaking without looking at Ellénore, I felt my ideas becoming vaguer and my resolve weakening" (VI, 50). As soon as one invokes resolve by name, it is no longer there. Or again: "I was oppressed by the words that I had just pronounced, and I believed only faintly in the promise that I had given" (IX, 70). That may be a peculiarity of Adolphe, but it is only the hyperbole of a widespread human characteristic. To think something, on the one hand, and to say it or write it or hear it or read it, on the other, are two very different acts. However, one might say, thoughts are verbal too, one does not think without words. Maybe so; but speech is something more than a simple series of words; it is composed of words addressed to others, whereas thought, even though verbal, is addressed only to oneself.

The second law concerning communication refers to the one who is speaking as well as to the one who hears, and one might call it the *law of reification*. It consists of the notion that words, when they touch on the feelings of the interlocutors, have the power to create what they refer to, or at least to transform it. Or, going back to Constant's formula itself, "We are such changeful creatures that the emotions we feign, we end up feeling" (VI, 48). All of Adolphe's love for Ellénore is sparked by a few words, initially formulated as a deliberate falsehood. "Besides, warmed as I was by my own style, I felt, as I finished writing, a little of the passion that I had sought to express with all possible force." And, an obstacle having appeared meanwhile, "Love, which one hour before I had applauded myself for feigning, I suddenly believed myself to feel in its full fury" (II, 23). The deceitful speech becomes true.

Every transaction of love, actually, obeys this law; Constant's characters know it and act accordingly. When Ellénore wants to protect herself from Adolphe's love, she initially tries to set aside the words that conveyed it. "She consented to receive me only rarely, [. . .]

with the commitment that I would never speak to her of love" (III, 28). Ellénore is being wary, for she knows that to accept the language is to accept the love itself; the words will soon create the reality. And that is what happens shortly thereafter. "She allowed me to paint my love for her; she became familiarized by degrees with this language. Soon she acknowledged to me that she loved me" (III, 29). Accept the language, accept the love: the distance between the two propositions is narrow. Adolphe acted no differently when he tried to end his relationship with Ellénore. "I congratulated myself when I was able to substitute words of affection, of friendship, of devotion, for those of love" (V, 43).

And again we have the example of Adolphe's meetings with the baron de T***. Adolphe knows perfectly well everything the baron tells him; but he had never heard it said, and it is the fact of these words having been spoken that becomes significant. "Those somber words, 'Between every form of success and you, there stands an insurmountable obstacle, and that obstacle is Ellénore,' reverberated around me" (VII, 56). It is not the novelty of the idea that strikes Adolphe, it is the sentence itself. By the very fact of its existence, the sentence changes the relation between him and Ellénore, which it was supposed to describe. In the same way, Adolphe repeated a thousand times (but without *saying* it) that he should leave Ellénore; one day, he announced to the baron: the whole situation has changed. "I had beseeched Heaven suddenly to raise between

Ellénore and me an obstacle which I could not overcome. This obstacle had arisen" (X, 72). The fact of having stated his decision, of having put it into words, changes its very nature.

In the inverse sense, if words create the reality that they formerly referred to fictitiously, then silence makes this same reality disappear. "Sorrows that I hid, I more or less forgot" (VI, 48). But we must point out again that this rule relates only to the interlocutors' feelings, not to the impersonal world that surrounds them; to believe otherwise would be to succumb to the illusions of magic. "Certain people believe that, if we did not speak about how things are, things would not be that way; they would happily burn as arsonists those who warn us that a fire is raging" (*Les Cent-Jours*, II, "Deuxième note," 264).

With regard to the psychical realities of beings in communication, however, an unsuspected responsibility weighs on their shoulders. One should not speak for the sake of speaking, and words are always more than words; one must be wary of the consequences of his own speech. Constant himself thus formulates what he calls Adolphe's "principal idea": to announce the danger that lies in "the simple practice of borrowing the language of love." Speaking this way, "one starts down a road whose end cannot be foreseen" ("Préface" to the second edition, 6).

Religion and Morality

The allocentric disposition or feeling of transcendence may take two forms, as we have seen above; this outward existence may or may not be incarnated in another human being. One form evokes love, devotion, or desire for glory; the other, nature and the Divine. The first of these two varieties is usually called moral feeling, the second, religious feeling. The feelings themselves, both equally transcendent, combine together harmoniously. That is not necessarily the case, however, with moral feeling and positive religions. What is the relationship between those two? Examining this question is one of Constant's principal motivations in his work on religion, which for a while he had planned to call by the revealing title, *Des rapports de la religion avec la morale chez les peuples de l'Antiquité* [On the Relationship between Religion and Morality among the Peoples of Antiquity] (*Journal*, September 6, 1804). After politics and love, religion in its turn allows us to observe the failures of modernity and to wonder about the means of overcoming them.

Morality, the Judge of Religion

Morality, in a very general sense — that is, going beyond personal interest — is a pure incarnation of the feeling of transcendence (of "the need for enthusiasm"). It is universal, a characteristic of mankind. "The relations of human societies being the same everywhere, moral law, which is the theory of these relations, is also the same everywhere" (*Religion*, IV, XII, 11, 492). This does not prevent some individuals from being less moral than others; some come closer to this ideal than others do. Morals are "revealed to every mind," but only "in the process of its elevation" (IV, XII, 12, 503). However positive religions, or forms of religion, unlike the general sentiment, are infinitely variable and they can be the products of interest as well of the religious feeling. One can use religion to try to connect with the infinite around us, like asking God for assistance in one's current affairs (thus magic, purely utilitarian, is a religion stripped of religious feeling, cf. I, II, 6, 324).

Religion, one might say, oscillates between disinterest and interest, between morals and politics. One of its two principal forms, that which requires the presence of a caste which serves it exclusively — the "sacerdotal religions" — is far more inclined toward compromising with politics than is the other, religion without a priesthood (which Constant prefers for this very reason). The first conclusion of his examination is thus negative: religion cannot serve as a basis for morals, and the more it is insulated from politics, the better. Constant does not completely condemn all forms of priesthood, for he knows that the constitution of "a sacerdotal caste" is inevitable; nevertheless, he warns against this caste's spontaneous tendency to serve its own interests above all, and to resist any thought of improvement. The second conclusion is positive: whereas religion cannot be the foundation of morals, morality will be the means that makes it possible to evaluate specific religions. The less interested and the farther from political power each one of them is, the closer it is to pure religious feeling. "Morals thus become a kind of touchstone, a standard against which religious concepts may be measured" (IV, XII, 2, 358). The more a religion's gods resemble moral man, the more they incarnate an ideal of justice and generosity, the more sophisticated is that religion. Religion should not submit to any interest, not even to that which consists in nourishing beauty, says Constant — thinking no doubt of Chateaubriand.

The Religious Need

On the question of religion, Constant's work plays the middle ground, neither unconditional approval nor radical condemnation. That helps us to understand one of Constant's difficulties in finishing it (the other relates to the choice between a historical account and a systematic exposition): the fact is that he changes his project in mid-course. Dropping the idea of writing a work showing the inanity of religions, in the spirit of Helveticus, he ends up becoming an apologist — not for such and such religion, certainly, but for the religious feeling itself. He makes things clear on several occasions, for instance in *Ma Vie*, and in a letter to Hochet:

> I am no longer an intrepid Philosopher, sure that there is nothing after this world, and so content with this world that he is delighted that there should be no other one. My work is a singular proof of what Bacon says, that a little science leads to atheism, and more science to religion (October 11, 1811).

Atheism now appears to him to be a state worse than religion. "I have my own little touch of religion. But it all takes the form of feelings, of vague emotions: it cannot be reduced to a system" (*Journal*, February 19, 1805). This diffuse religiosity is not incompatible with doubt: "We experience doubt as much as and more than anyone else; but doubt does not exclude the religious feeling" (*Religion*, V, XV, 1, 172).

One can thus distinguish several levels in Constant's reflection on religion. As far as immediate experience is concerned, and aside from two episodes during which he seeks consolation for his sentimental difficulties in piety, he leaves it to uncertainty, therefore to agnosticism, rather than to atheism. "I am too much a skeptic to be a non-believer," he states to Rosalie (on November 15, 1829). One should not conclude that religion is harmful, because of its abuses. "To be made a non-believer because insane or malicious people have misused religion, is to make oneself a eunuch because the libertines have come down with syphilus" (to Prosper de Barante, October 11, 1811). Any categorical assertion is thus to be dismissed. There is, secondly, a progression of religious forms, from fetishism to polytheism, and from there to monotheism, a progression that consists in purifying religion of any immediate interest and also in removing cosmological speculation into physics. Finally, there may be a progressive liberation from the priesthood. If Christianity is higher than the other religions, it is because it represents a decisive step in this passage toward purification that makes it possible to transfer the religious experience from society to the individual. "Religion has withdrawn from the external life; but it has become all the stronger within man" (to the same , October 21, 1808). From this point of view, Constant remains faithful to his Protestant origins.

This improved religion is close to the creed professed by the Savoyard Vicar, imagined by Rousseau in *Emile*. But, at the same time, Constant does not wish to see the love of God replaced by a religion of humanity, like Auguste Comte. For him (and that is what separates him from the atheists), the religious feeling has to do with our relationship to the invisible, not with the relationship we have with our peers, and this feeling cannot be eradicated; it is part of humanity's trans-historic identity.

If that is the case, what will be the religion of the future? Constant is as hostile to theocracy, when religion seizes political power, as he is to the modern ideocracy in which a reason of State is transformed into a religion. He imagines something resembling more a lay State where the central power would ensure everyone's right to practice his own religion. Rather than having to choose among religions, why not accommodate them all, only taking care that they be contained inside the private sphere of the individual and thus that they do not lead to new wars of religion? "This multiplicity of sects, which is so terrifying to some, is what would be most salutary for religion" (*Principes*, 1806, VIII, 3, 165). This religious pluralism (which is obviously not a return to polytheism) not only conforms with the liberal politics of separation between what is private and what is public, it is also conducive to the improvement of religion itself and to its influence on society. "Divide the torrent, or even better, let it be divided into a thousand brooks. They will fertilize the ground which the torrent would have devastated" (*Religion*, V, XV, 4, 207). Adolphe defends the same opinion, from a more interested point of view:

> My surprise is not that man needs a religion; what astonishes me is that he ever believes himself strong

enough, sheltered enough from misfortune, to dare to
reject even one of them. It seems to me that he should,
in his weakness, be induced to call upon them all; in the
dense night that surrounds us, is there any glimmer we
can do without? (X, 77-78).

Faith, the Basis of Morality

This first articulation of the relationship between
morality and religion does not yet cover everything.
When he returns to the perspective of public life, Constant sees a problem in the contemporary deterioration
of religion. The life of a society rests on all its members'
implicit acceptance of the same social contract. "The
great and difficult problem of society consists in discovering a sanction for men's commitments between themselves" (*Religion*, I, II, 3, 275). No interaction is possible
if we do not share this minimal reciprocal confidence.
Religion, by introducing a supernatural dimension into
human existence, makes it possible to regard this contract as sacred and thus to found it: the oath is a commitment before God, and not only before men. The immortality of the soul makes us fear punishment in the
beyond, even if we escape it during mortal life. If religion is withdrawn, the contract is no longer guaranteed
and is threatened by a war of all against all:

> Then all the bonds are broken. Right no longer exists;
> duty disappears with right; force is unchained; perjury
> places society in a permanent state of war and fraud

(276).

To be moral is, first of all, to be able to give preference to others over oneself. Imagining the extreme case, one should thus say: to be moral is to be able to sacrifice oneself, to find values higher than one's own life. "The power of sacrifice," as Constant calls it, is "the mother of all virtue" (*Madame de Staël,* 222). But why prefer something over one's own life, if you think this life is the only one that exists? "What is there greater than life, for those who see only nothingness in the beyond?" (*Religion,* I, I, 4, 89) If such is the case, why risk one's life, why not seek to extract from it the maximum immediate pleasure? If God is dead, isn't everything permissible?

> If life is only, in the final analysis, a bizarre apparition without a future or a past, and so short that it would scarcely be considered real, what good is it to sacrifice oneself to the principles whose application is distant at best? Better to enjoy every hour, doubtful as we are that another hour will follow, and to intoxicate oneself with every pleasure while pleasure is possible (88-89).

In writing the chilling pages in which he describes the degradation of atheistic society, Constant was undoubtedly inspired by his observations of mores under Napoleon. But for us, his descriptions testify to a strange prescience, as if one were reading an anticipated evocation of the behaviors in the totalitarian societies of the 20th century. Non-belief destroys all the virtues, and neither does it even represent liberation.

"When the whip of the inquisitors is raised, this rabble of non-believers gets back on its knees at the alter, and atheism begs, on its way out of the temple, for the wages of hypocrisy." Subservience to temporal power justifies all forms of turpitude. "Adulation, calumny, lowness pretend to be innocent, claiming to have been compelled. Everyone who claims to have been forced holds himself to be absolved" (90). One thinks he excuses himself by publicly making fun of himself, by showing his cynicism. "They laugh at their own slavery and their own corruption, without being less slaves, or less corrupt" (91). To substitute the power of the State, or positive laws, for religion as the basis for morals thus hardly advances us.

Here is what awaits us if we stop believing in immortality. Only the religious inclination gives us this faith. "This alone, by increasing the value of life, by surrounding it with an atmosphere of immortality, makes this life itself a possible object of sacrifice" (II, V, 7, 485). Could we count on pure morals, stripped of any link to religion? We already know Constant's pessimism in this regard: few are they who can rise above their interests, few are the moments when each of us does so. "The mass of mankind" cannot, should not, try to get by without religion (V, XV, 1, 172). Morals without religion, according to Constant, remain purely disincarnated; reduced to dry duty, it gives off "an aura of sadness," its atmosphere is "somber and severe" (*Polythéisme*, I, VII, 1, 204). Religion clothes its principles in beautiful and concrete forms, which make them attractive to all; it translates them into the narrative and picturesque language of tradition. But what can we do today, at the very time that religion is dying and faith no longer reigns?

"Morals require time," affirms Constant (*Conquête*, I, 5, 96) — that is to say, a reference to life after death. Ancient peoples used means other than religion to achieve this — they believed in the value of glory, which is located not within us but outside ourselves, including in the following generations. This is why Achilles, the ancient hero, preferred glorious death to life without glory. But the men of modern times, the era of the individual, have given up seeking glory and are satisfied with their private pleasures. We should not be deluded on this point. "What we are missing, and what we should miss, are conviction, enthusiasm and the power to sacrifice interest to opinion" (*Religion*, I, "Préface ", XLI).

Human Love, Divine Love

One might wonder whether Constant is not taking his argument a little too far, carried away as he is by his apologia for religious feeling, and whether he is not forgetting the line that others of his pages suggest. Is faith in immortality, and therefore religion, the only possible basis of transcendence? On the contrary, doesn't the awareness of death impel us, as he says elsewhere, to seek beyond the surface of things? Moreover, don't we all know another form of transcendence, much closer to hand, which overtakes our life not in time but in space, at every moment — that which is represented by others for every *I*? Constant writes:

> The idea of sacrifice [. . .] is inseparable from any profound and heartfelt affection. Love takes pleasure in sacrificing, to the being that it prefers, everything else that it holds dear (I, II, 2, 250).

And when, at the beginning of his book, he refers to other forms of the allocentric disposition, after religious feeling he enumerates: love, enthusiasm, sympathy, devotion ("Préface," XXVIII). But if authentic love and the other affections illustrate daily the capacity of sacrifice, we might ask Constant, why do we need immortality? Rather than relying on life after death, can't we rely on these beings which exist apart from us and who nonetheless form a part of us, whose happiness creates ours? Even if we have only one life, and it is terminated at the moment of our death, can we conclude that we are not condemned to set up this finite life as the supreme value, since there is continuity between what is internal and what is external: sociability replaces immortality.

Constant does not confuse human love and divine love; however, he remains sensitive to that which they have in common. Both going beyond the bounds of the individual person, they enable us to overcome the discouragement that is born from consciousness of our own finitude. The religious feeling is valuable above all for the contact that it enables us to establish with the infinite. "The absence of limits applied to our feelings and to our thoughts is that which most tends to purify some and to elevate the others." But in its turn love helps us to experience this sense of the infinite. "Love is ennobled, love is purified, only because as long as it lasts it believes it will never end" (*Polythéisme*, II, XVIII, 3, 311). The objection that lovers only deceive themselves and that real loves are anything but eternal does not apply here; what counts is the subject's intimate feeling and the concrete experience of the infinite, which he feels in this manner. The feelings which we can devote to each other help us, indeed, to discover transcendence.

We who live two centuries after Constant can confirm it. In the absence of religious sanction, the social contract does not break down, men do not begin to live in the state of a war of all against all — for they are preserved from it by their very sociability, by their permanent need to live with other people. The apocalypse sometimes imagined by Constant has not occurred, except in totalitarian countries where the confiscation of social relations by the State has transformed individuals into beings who only have interests. Where social life has been allowed to follow its own laws, in other words, in democracy, it appears that morals do not rest only upon the only fear of sanctions, natural or supernatural.

But we would betray Constant if we allowed morals to supplant religion entirely. For him, religion holds an irreducible place. Only, the religion of democratic man is not that which reigned in traditional societies. Once again, Constant rejects materialism, which appears simplistic to him, as well as the pure and simple reproduction of the institution as we inherited it. To be precise, religion must cease being an institution, as much as possible, and become only an internal feeling that connects man to all that is unknown to him, all that transcends him and keeps him from being totally self-centered. The religious is our relationship with the invisible, our non-coincidence with ourselves; it begins as soon as we leave the realm of material need. In this sense, our relations to others also become part of this religious sphere and it is not by chance if human love acquires the attributes of divine love: the one enlightens the other.

Compassion

Other People's Suffering

Constant does not linger on the possibility of founding morality in lateral transcendence, in that continuity that others form with us. He examines in detail only one of the types of this means of going beyond oneself, and that is pity, the sympathy elicited by other people's pain. He even proposes, in this context, to seek the origin of the virtues not in sacrifice, or the going beyond oneself, but in suffering. There are two varieties of suffering — one that we experience ourselves, and one that we see in others — thus giving rise to two types of virtue, those of the *I* and those depending on *you*:

> It is through pain that man is improved. [. . .] Pain sometimes awakens the noble side of our nature, cour-

age, as well as tenderness, sympathy and pity. It teaches us to fight for ourselves, and to feel for others (*Religion*, IV, XI, 5, 269).

And, in his own life, Constant would always recognize this constructive role of suffering. "Misfortune gives an occasion for the development of a thousand qualities that we never suspected in each other and for which we will be grateful throughout our lives" (to the countess of Nassau, September 19, 1808).

What interests Constant above all is the suffering of others or, more precisely, the chord that it strikes in us. In that, he follows not so much Rousseau as the Christian doctrines, which accord a central place to pity, in that context called charity:

Charity is nothing more or less than a sensitivity so exalted by fear of pain that pain becomes no less unbearable to contemplate in others than to feel in oneself (*Passions religieuses*, 284).

The neighbor, in the parable of the good Samaritan, is neither the person who is socially close to us, nor man in general, but a being that is defined by suffering: someone is in distress and for this reason he needs his "neighbor."

Constant views this thought to be the starting point of our humanity, in that compassion is experienced in relation to the suffering of others. "Misfortune was, for us, like Prometheus' fire," he writes in an unpublished manuscript. Why? Because "misfortune created sympathy" (*Perfectibilité*, II, 692).   Animals do not suffer from the suffering of others:

> Man then sprang from the midst of the animals, and became a moral being. The germ of perfectibility was developed. For everything in man that is generous and great is based on the principle of sympathy, that is, on the impossibility of contemplating another's pain with- out emotion, and on the need to help (693).

The editor of *Adolphe* draws the conclusion from this axiom: if what is best in us consists in helping oth- ers in their misfortune, then what is worst is causing that misfortune:

> The great question in life is the pain that we cause, and the cleverest metaphysics does not justify the man who shatters the heart that loved him ("Réponse," 82-83).

Constant certainly seems to conduct his life accord- ing to this principle, particularly in the ten years (1800- 1811) during which he would like to leave Germaine de Staël but does not dare to, for fear of making her suffer. The first result of this choice is the suspension of any action. He writes to Anna Lindsay, at the height of their passion: "We must wait until we can unite ourselves without wounding any being who has the right to expect us to avoid causing sor- row" (December 22, 1800). But don't they run the risk of having to wait a long time? Doesn't any choice in love cause, in principle, unhappiness for those who are not selected? How can one take a step in life without ever "risking unhappiness or trouble to another" (to Rosalie Constant, May 29, 1803)? We must accept our limits, not only in time but in space — no one can make everyone happy at the same time. Caught in the interlacing of multiple human relationships, one is obliged to establish hierarchies, and thus to cause unhappiness. Montaigne was right to recall, in the title of one of his essays, this ancient wisdom — what is good for one is bad for another. Rousseau agreed: people are communicating vessels, we "make one person happy at the cost of making a hundred miserable" (*Emile*, II, 340). Can intimate life as a whole be submitted only to compassion? On a day of discouragement, Constant comes up with this formula: "I only love in absence, out of gratitude and pity" (*Journal*, September 22, 1813). In other words, either the logic of desire ("in absence") or that of duty ("of gratitude") or compassion. But that was on a day when he no longer believed in the social life: "My heart lives alone," said the preceding sentence.

Adopting this line of behavior for the whole central period of his life, Constant lived in a permanent state of indecision and hesitation. The narrator of *Ma Vie* blesses the circumstance that imposes a decision on him: "I breathed freely again, now that I knew my own mind" (121). Meanwhile, the narrator of *Cécile* appeals, in vain, to Providence:

> Buffeted by a storm of contrary thoughts, I went again, in my memory, over the long series of inconsistencies of which

I had made myself guilty; [. . .] reduced to choosing between unavoidable evils, I called upon Heaven to guide me (VII, 183).

So that Cécile is forced to challenge him: "I entreat you to look inside and finally to know yourself" (VI, 177). But is that even possible, if the truth of the being is in its dependence on the context and the degree of suffering that it can cause or avoid in every person that he meets?

By this stage, Constant is so accustomed to his own hesitations that, when he decides one day to keep an encoded diary, he sees he will be obliged to assign a number to every decision and to its opposite, knowing from experience that he will need both:

2. Desire to break my eternal bond, which is so often in question. 3. Return to this bond through memories, or some temporary charm. [. . .] 5. Argument with my father. 6. Tenderness toward my father. [. . .] 9. Tired of Mme. Lindsay. 10. Sweet memories and inclination again toward Mme. Lindsay. 11. Wavering in my plans with regard to Mme. Du Tertre. 12. Love for Mme. Du Tertre.

And, as if he knew that this attempt to ward off uncertainty by codifying it would be condemned to failure, he adds, in despair: "13. Uncertainty about everything" (May 12, 1808).

Constant is well aware of the disadvantages of his own obsession for the misfortune of others, but he does not manage to overcome it. He wonders in the *Journal:*

> Is there a reason for the sadness of a person whom I do
> not make happy at all, while sacrificing myself for her?
> I am agitated with quivers of a miserable weakness of
> character. Never was there anything more ridiculous
> than my indecision. Sometimes marriage, sometimes
> solitude, sometimes Germany, sometimes France, hesi-
> tant on all fronts because, fundamentally, I could do
> without any of them (on August 1, 1804).

Could uncertainty be a mask for indifference? To
avoid causing Germaine pain (and fury), Benjamin is no
longer satisfied with sacrificing his own happiness, he
must also sacrifice that of the other women who love
him, especially, from 1807 on, Charlotte: in spite of their
secret marriage in 1808, in spite of its officialization in
1809, Benjamin continues to live with Germaine until
1811! Pity, from a noble moral principle, seems to have
become a personal pathology. It pursues him, it torments him, to the point of paralyzing all his faculties.

This explanation of his behavior with Germaine
(followed, it should be said, by several others) crops up
in his correspondence and in the *Journal* with the insis-
tence of a litany. He can no longer say that he would be
happy to make this woman happy. All that remains of
his love is this: knowing that she is unhappy, and moreover through his fault, not only makes his happiness
impossible, but unbearable for him. To cause pain in
others produces in him "an anguish that drives [him]
insane" (to Rosalie Constant, November 14, 1809). This
suffering is worse than direct pain: "One suffers much

more for others than for oneself" (to the countess of Nassau, April 20, 1807). From this, Constant deduces a principle for action: pain should be respected, and ideally one would act in such a way as to cause the least possible harm. "I am convinced that true morality is to spare people from pain to the greatest possible extent" (to the same person, July 12, 1808). He is quick to make any sacrifice that may help him toward this goal. Pursuing his own happiness is no longer possible if that must cause unhappiness to others. Here, Constant remains faithful to the lesson of Julie in *La Nouvelle Héloise*, who said: "It will be less painful to me to wail in my own sorrows than to have caused theirs" (that of her parents: II, 6, 209).

Dominated by Pain

One may wonder, again, whether this profuse and monotonous speech on the refusal to cause pain is not intended to mask a more difficult admission (or more inaccessible to Constant himself): his self-reproach for having "left" and killed his own mother at the same time, at the moment of his birth — his panic at the prospect of any separation in love, as if it would mean his own death. To leave is to kill. Little Benjamin killed his mother by leaving her, Adolphe kills Ellénore in the same way. Constant describes his obsession with separations in a letter to Prosper de Barante:

These break-ups, which appear extremely simple as

> long as the objects still exist, become awfully lugubrious when they are ended by that great and silent catastrophe that puts an end to everything (April 22, 1808).

To make other people's pain the touchstone of any moral action means to head down a dubious path: must I regret the suffering of the envious? Should I not condemn evil, even if nobody suffers from it in the immediate future? "We do not hate the malicious only because they harm us; but because they are malicious," Rousseau observed (*Emile*, IV, 597). The approach that Constant recommends is all the more problematic since we now know how fluid are human emotions and how little confidence one can place in the words that express the feelings. Speaking to his cousin Rosalie about his obligations towards Germaine, Benjamin declares that he will not be able to leave her "as long as I believe her to be of good faith in her pain and her sentiments" (November 14, 1809). But how can we verify someone's good faith? Even more, is there, in regard to feelings, a clear border between good and bad faith? Is absolute sincerity even possible? How can we distinguish it from emotional blackmail, from intentionally making others feel guilty, from deliberately choosing the victim's role to ensure our privileged position vis à vis the one whom we hold responsible for our misfortune? Constant himself resorts to suicide attempts several times in order to achieve his goals: you are the one who is responsible for my suffering, he seems to say by his gesture, and only you can cure it. Doesn't Germaine do as much herself? "She persists in saying that she will commit suicide if I leave her. I do not believe a word of it, but it is dreadful to hear" (*Journal*, July 10, 1807). Even gentle Charlotte tries it, when faced with her husband's indecision to move in with her!

Constant's thoughts on the matter do not mesh with his own experience, which is reflected in his personal writings. In *Adolphe,* subservience to other people's pain is recommended by the Editor but not by the story line itself. Ellénore's suffering turns into more or less deliberate manipulation of Adolphe. Ellénore seeks to paralyze him with the spectacle of her pain, itself proved by everything that she has already sacrificed to him. Sacrifice ceases being synonymous with a value higher than life itself, and becomes a quasi-mechanical means of causing pity and preventing the break-up. "She had sacrificed everything for me, fortune, children, reputation; she demanded no other payment for her sacrifices but to wait for me like a humble slave" (V, 45). Isn't such a description enough to announce the tragic outcome of the story? The more one sacrifices, the more one has the right to demand; self-sacrifice thus is by no means the attitude of a humble slave, it is, on the contrary, the most effective way to become the one who is entitled to reparations. It is Adolphe who is now the subjected one. "As soon as I saw an expression of pain on her face, her will would become mine" (IV, 34).

The entire history of their relationship is punctuated by new sacrifices by Ellénore, which become as many new chains for Adolphe. Upon the least hesitation on his part, she reminds him that she will be taken — because of him! — "for an ungrateful daughter and an uncaring mother," that she "sacrificed [her] entire life" and that, especially, "you accepted it, this sacrifice" (VI, 5, 1). Isn't the acceptance of such an immense gift tantamount to becoming forever indebted to the one who made the sacrifice? Ellénore dominates Adolphe by her pain, and by it alone (VII, 58), and he knows that every ill-considered gesture is likely to cause "a new sacrifice" (VI, 52) and that upon each new suffering she could throw in his face, "But it is your fault" (VIII, 63). The more Ellénore presents herself as a victim, the more she gains rights (VIII, 67) and the more Adolphe feels guilty. She is not satisfied to commit suicide, she does better: she takes care to let him know, after her death, that he is the only one responsible! Should we be astonished that, consequently, crushed under this weight, Adolphe never succeeded in engaging in a new life?

While thus displaying his adherence to the doctrine of pity ruling over life, Constant shows us, by the unfolding events in his novel, the dead end to which this road leads. It is good to worry about the suffering of individuals rather than the purity of principles, and Mme. de Staël, who acted in this spirit, deserves unreserved praise. But to go from there to making it the governing principle of life is a line that Constant discreetly recommends to us not to cross, even if his obsessions do not always leave him the freedom to follow his own precepts. Human commerce, with its plurality in simultaneity and its impossibility of complete sincerity, cannot be governed by such a law; and that applies not only in public life, where justice for all is higher than compassion for suffering individuals, but also in personal life.

Three Narratives

Today, only three of Constant's more literary texts remain: a short novel, *Adolphe*, and two unfinished and even shorter autobiographical accounts, *Cécile* and *Ma Vie*. In paperback edition they make up barely 200 pages altogether. The novel's brevity and density give the effect of a logical argument; but what does it prove, exactly?

Impossible Love

From the start, *Adolphe* places us in a world from which the absolute, in its traditional forms, has disappeared. God is absent, even if one may address appeals to him, and with him the idea of immortality has disappeared. All of life occurs here and now. Death is close at hand, all around us, certain and irreversible; men, through lack of concern or through anguish, endeavor to ignore it. As for Adolphe, he thinks of it constantly and comes to this conclusion: since one's existence will come to an end, one must be resigned to living without any absolutes, with concerns only for the moment. "I preferred to read those poets who comment on the brevity of human life. I found that no aim was worth the trouble of any effort" (I, 15).

But isn't it possible that a purely human notion of the sacred could take the place of the supernatural sacred? That is the ambition of love. By making a gift of his person to others, by cherishing *others* more than himself, one attains once more a world that exceeds finitude. When Adolphe and Ellénore fall in love for the first time, he sees in her "something touching, something sacred," and he warns himself: "Woe to man who, in the first moments of a love affair, does not believe that this connection must be eternal (III, 32)." Emotional attachments transcend ordinary existence, with its prosaic sequences of means and ends. Human love replaces divine love in its function as an absolute.

The two sexes react differently to love. In *Adolphe*'s time as in ours, men are engaged in public life; they have material or political ambitions which appear to them to be legitimate goals in life; they are aware of love but often believe that their principal destiny is to play a certain role in society. Women, excluded for the most part from public life by society's rules, make love much more the center of their existence. They have "the noble and dangerous faculty of living through another and for another" ("Préface" of the second edition, 6). This faculty is noble: it overcomes the logic of egoistic interest and thus reintroduces the sacred into life. It is more than noble, it is right. Nobody can live without others. In this respect, Constant too "is" a woman. The ongoing consideration given to others' points of view, which Rousseau ascribed to the female kind, Constant assumes without hesitation. He is at the same time Émile and Sophie, Adolphe and Ellénore. It is thus not only a faculty, it is also a need — however, at the same time, it is dangerous. Why?

Because men and women are finite beings and sentiments are, in turn, mortal; therefore the situation is doubly dangerous. Not only can love come to an end in one party or the other, and thereby cause suffering; but also, if all of life is guided by this new form of the sacred, it breaks into pieces when love is over. Then mistrust is born, which, "forced to direct itself against the one being that had been elevated above all others, extends then to the rest of the world" (7). The center being lost, everything collapses; one finds oneself rejected to the fringes of life. For us simple mortals, love is the only absolute; however, love itself is not reliable. Thus we are condemned to unhappiness. Such seems to be the theorem that *Adolphe* proves. But why does love fail? Is it really inevitable? The story tries to convince us that it is.

In its first chapters, *Adolphe* can be read as a perfect illustration of the logic of desire; love is defined as a lack. The natural order of things would call for the hero, this new Valmont, this libertine from the novels of Laclos or Crébillon, to turn around and leave as soon as the conquest is consummated. However, he cannot; he stays. Here appears the second great principle that underlies human actions (or at least those of Adolphe) — compassion. Adolphe cannot bear the thought of causing other people's suffering. A new absolute emerges: "Anyone who suffers because he loves is sacred" ("Préface" of the second edition, 7). The Editor's final "*Réponse*" repeats it: nothing can offset that suffering.

This principle may be beautiful, but implementing it is problematical. Concerning Ellénore, one quickly comes to suspect that, knowing in advance how Adolphe will react, she deliberately chooses suffering. Her behavior is a series of sacrifices: she gives up her former lover, her children, her father, society, fortune! After each sacrifice, her suffering could only grow if Adolphe dared to leave her. All of Ellénore's misfortunes are Adolphe's fault; he is paralyzed. He knows that it is no longer love but pity that holds him to her. That does not matter; he stays. Adolphe's only option is to take on the role of victim in turn, to add up his own sacrifices, but this raising of the stakes does not release them from each other.

Throughout most of the book, Adolphe is unhappy living with Ellénore because he does not love her enough. There are two possible solutions to this: either to leave Ellénore, or to love her more. However, he cannot do either one. He is immobilized; he does not move in either direction, and satisfies himself with imploring Heaven to decide for him. He cannot leave Ellénore, for to make her suffer is unbearable. Eventually, his fears prove justified: his leaving does cause Ellénore's death and inflicts upon Adolphe an ineffaceable culpability. But why can't he love her more?

Adolphe knows what true love is like. "Her happiness was necessary for me, and I knew I was necessary to her happiness" (IV, 35), but he does not manage to keep himself in this state. Public opinion is one of the reasons that make their love impossible. Ellénore is a fallen woman because she never married the father of her children; her social status is inferior to Adolphe's. However, he knows very well that this difficulty would be surmountable if only he had sufficient will. It is in himself that the incapacity to love resides. What is it that made it so? We do not know, but one may be struck by the fact that, when he recapitulates his life in the first chapter, he never mentions his mother. Adolphe has only a father, who is not at all maternal: no demonstration of affection is possible with him. The young Adolphe that we discover only knows how to make "solitary plans," and considers "even the presence of others an annoyance and an obstacle." What animates him constantly is "a burning desire for independence, a great impatience with the bonds by which I was surrounded, an invincible terror of forming any new ones" (I, 14). And throughout the entire account that follows, he will complain about "ties" and will aspire to greater "independence." Those who surround him are struck by his "inexplicable thirst for breaking away and for isolation" (VIII, 61). However, left alone, Adolphe is not satisfied either. He soon discovers that the other name for independence is the desert of the world, the absence of love, painful loneliness; and the "Lettre à l'Editeur" teaches us that, after Ellénore's death, he scarcely enjoyed this independence.

Adolphe wants relationships, and yet they terrorize him. This terror reaches a degree that remains mysterious. Everyone, undoubtedly, hopes for and at the same time fears love; but, for Adolphe, terror wins out and paralyzes his own capacities to love, as if he feared that no real love can fill the emptiness from which he suffers. He is pained by it himself but can't do anything about it. The will is impotent in the face of love. "To revive a feeling that has died out, what good is a resolution taken out of obligation?" (V, 41). These are two spheres that do not communicate. And that is why Adolphe appealed to Heaven, asking for guidance in his actions.

However, Constant wanted to present this impossibility of loving not as a personal incapacity of Adolphe, but as the law of human commerce:

> He and Ellénore had no recourse, and that is precisely what I wanted. I showed him tormented, because he only loved Ellénore a little; but he would not have been less tormented if he had loved her more. For want of feeling, he suffered through her; with a more passionate feeling, he would have suffered for her ("Préface" to the second edition, 8).

But that means reducing any love to the logic of desire: one loves only because one is not loved, one ceases loving as soon as the other loves in return. However, Adolphe's own behavior, never mind that of other men, does not reflect this mechanics exclusively. In the abandoned preface to *Adolphe,* Constant seemed to mark a greater distance from the tragic dilemma in which his characters are locked. He associated the incapacity to love with other forms of specifically modern decadence, the demise of faith and will, by evoking the deficit of such positive forms of character. "Fidelity in love is a force, like religious belief, like the passion for freedom" (196). All of Constant's thoughts lead us to reject this resignation before the allegedly inevitable evils of modernity. Happy love exists, even if it is seldom found.

But this happy love has no place in the literary form chosen by Constant. The novel is always inspired by other genres; it absorbs them and transforms them, and the same is true of the epic and the biography. In France, tragedy provides the model for the most prestigious works, *La Princesse de Clèves, Manon Lescaut, Les Liaisons dangereuses* and so many others. Like them, *Adolphe* tells the story of an impossible happiness, of an inevitable misfortune; it can only end in failure and death. What distinguishes it, on the other hand, is the insignificant role reserved for external events, with the exception of Ellénore's death. The rest of the time, one has the impression that the characters are satisfied to carry on an idle existence, deprived of any vivid action, that they go from one city to another as easily as from cocktails to dinner. Constant wanted to show that "circumstances are of no consequence, character is everything" (*Adolphe*, "Réponse," 83; he wrote also to Prosper de Barante, June 9, 1808: "The facts are the least of our problems"). These beings have only a verbal existence: conversations, letters, soliloquies. On the other hand, Constant discovered the infinite complexity of the word, and never tires of analyzing it: the word that, far from being a flexible and transparent reflection of the world, creates it or destroys it, masks or prepares it; the word that gives life and death.

How would one organize such a novel where the situation, as Constant says, always stays the same? *Adolphe* is constructed as a theme with variations. As a theme, we have the great principles: love as lack, imperious compassion, fear of personal ties. The variations come as a series of tiny events illustrating sometimes the one, sometimes the other. The overall order is symmetrical: immobility in the first chapter, and a portrait of the narrator; the heightening of sentiments in chapters 2 and 3, leading to an exclamatory paragraph at the beginning of chapter 4, which describes happy love — while declaring that this description is impossible; and from then on, a progressive degradation of love, leading to Ellénore's death in chapter 10. The tale is told in the first person, and it is not a simple narrative: introspection, never taken so far before, is the wellspring of this inquiry which, with its pitiless demand for clarity, often calls to mind a private diary. The whole is framed by the remarks of an imaginary Editor, who describes Adolphe to us from the outside by providing some information on his later destiny. This Editor is not Constant (who addresses us in the prefaces) and his interpretations are not to be taken literally.

The text of *Adolphe* is made up of two types of statements: sentences in the past tense, which bring back events or features of character, their behaviors and motives, and sentences in the present tense, which formulate timeless adages, such as:

> Almost always, in order to live comfortably with ourselves, we disguise as calculations and systems our powerlessness, our inabilities and our weaknesses. In that way we satisfy the portion of us that is, so to speak, the spectator of the other (II, 22).

La Rochefoucauld could have put his name to this maxim, for the form as for the content. What we perceive as Constant's lucidity is the tendency to explain seemingly noble or at least innocent actions by far less admissible egoistic reasons. In that, he is close to the moralists of the 17th century. But other features of his style, by contrast, bring him very close to us today. He despises emphasis, effusive feelings, posing. He is much farther from *La Nouvelle Héloïse* or the prose of Chateaubriand than from the Civil Code that was so dear to Stendhal, who, it should be remembered, was known to praise "the extreme truth" of *Adolphe* (206). There are no descriptions, either of nature or of interiors, except purely functional; no social or historical context. The drama is played out only within the private life. The style is as pared down as the tale: nothing superfluous encumbers it. This does not mean that *Adolphe* is a simple text. A central mystery lives within it, and with each reading one discovers new layers. Constant was not satisfied to illustrate a thesis that one could dispute; he brought to life two individuals caught in the unfolding of a story. The meaning of this tale is inexhaustible.

Constant's sole novel is described as a masterpiece; one can understand why. The simplicity and the universality of the major themes, their tragic intricacies, the narrative and stylistic rigor, all contribute to the same end. The very brevity of the book accentuates the impression of determinism: nothing excessive, only that which is essential in leading to the final catastrophe. Constant seems to read the unhappy love affair with the deductive rigor of a geometrician.

Between Two Women

Cécile, on the other hand, proposes to tell the story of a happy love. This autobiographical account, where Constant nevertheless takes the precaution of changing the characters' names and where he deviates sometimes from the factual truth, must indeed relate the story of the author and his second wife, Charlotte (called here Cécile), from their first meeting to the present marital happiness. It seems to have been written around 1810. But, by chance or by necessity, Constant interrupts its narration at a moment that is not at all happy; so that one departs from *Cécile*, in its final state, with a new account of impossible loves!

Several features of the text recall *Adolphe*. The logic of desire as lack is again at work here, in particular in the beginning (the first "epoch" of *Cécile* is rigorously parallel to chapter 2 of *Adolphe*). The narrator remains lucid as to the hidden or inadmissible motives of allegedly virtuous actions, his own as well as those of the others. He is still very attentive to linguistic attitudes and describes the infinitesimal nuances of feelings, he knows how to show their "mobility," the facility with which they change, when placed in contact with each other. His language remains simple and precise.

The characters here are more complex than those in *Adolphe*. In the place of Ellénore, desired but then little loved, unhappy and exploiting her own sacrifices, one finds two types of women. One is the woman of spirit, equal to man on the intellectual level and endowed with a dominating nature. In the beginning of the story it was Mme. de Chenevière, in other words Mme. de Charrière, who was also evoked in *Adolphe*, but far more briefly; and later Mme. de Malbée, i.e. Mme. de Staël, with whom the narrator lives in spiritual communion but who subjugates him on all other planes. "I had never seen anything like that in the whole world. I fell passionately in love" (II, 149). Note that Constant does not say here, as he did in relation to Cécile and Ellénore, "I thought I was experiencing love." "Her spirit dazzled me, her gaiety enchanted me, her praises turned my head. At the end of an hour, she held over me the most unlimited dominion that a woman perhaps ever exerted" (III, 150). Adolphe never saw anything like that.

The other type of woman, embodied by Cécile, illustrates an almost maternal passion. The relationship starts with seduction, like that of Adolphe and Ellénore; but on the other hand Cécile does not have any of Ellénore's handicaps. She is legally married, she is noble and rich, and she does not have children. Therefore, she will not have to sacrifice her reputation, her fortune or her maternal love; she will never play that card. In a flash, she decides that the narrator will be man of her life and that she will continue to love him no matter what he does and no matter how long it takes him to join her. This unconditional love wins out over the narrator's reservations and, as we learn from the first lines of the story, he will become Cécile's happy husband.

Cécile, which follows the vicissitudes of a biography, cannot have the geometrical rigor of *Adolphe*. But the succession of events, grouped in "epochs," is not chaotic either. At the beginning we have the meeting, the initial fascination. Then, various obstacles or accidents keep the two apart. They find each other again nearly twelve years later; their feelings revive, they become lovers and decide to marry. Then begins a new decline in their relationship, taking up the end of the sixth and the seventh (unfinished) epoch. The tone changes from sprightly to solemn. The narrative is interrupted in the midst of hesitation, and it is difficult to imagine how it can lead to a happy ending.

The reasons for these new difficulties are not external; they reside in the very character of the narrator. He and Cécile are both, at the moment of their promise to marry, committed to other people. The narrator is the (unhappy) companion of Mme. de Malbée, Cécile has remarried and will have to divorce again. But only the narrator creates problems. In contrast to Adolphe, his indecision is not between two principles, but between two women, Mme. de Malbée and Cécile.

The narrator of *Cecile* shares certain impulses of the heart with Adolphe. Like him, he has known "the passion for independence" (II, 146); but, at the moment of his current hesitation, there is no question of what now seems like an adolescent aspiration. He finds it difficult to choose between two relationships, not between their presence and their absence. Like Adolphe, he fears "the specter of Mme. de Malbée's pain" (VI, 169), but he is not easily deceived; he knows that suffering, even when sincere, is converted at once into emotional blackmail, and that enables him to resist Mme. de Malbée's spectacular demonstrations of distress. The narrator does not doubt that his life would be sweeter with Cécile. Finally he knows that, by his inability to choose, he produces "the unhappiness of two women," and that overwhelms him. However, he remains unable to decide and, in his turn, begs Heaven to choose — convinced, once more, that it is a matter of choosing between "inescapable evils" (VII, 183). Why these "strange vacillations" (II, 148)?

In the final analysis, after having eliminated many partial answers, he arrives at the following explanation:

> An affair of thirteen years was thus going to be terminated. I was going to give up a woman to whom I had given, from whom I had received, so many signs of affection. She had been the tyrant, but she had also been the purpose of my life. A thousand memories were intertwined around my heart; all that I had done for her, the devotion that I had testified to her were going to be lost. I was going to throw far away from me all the good that I had been able to do in more than a third of my existence (VII, 180).

Clearly, the narrator is not, according to the usual logic of desire, in the process of idealizing the object of love because he is going to lose it. He does not represent Mme. de Malbée as better than she is. What he regrets is not really her, but his own past. A being is nothing other than its existence; to separate from a person also means leaving, and thus losing, a part of one's own identity. This mourning is what the narrator does not manage to complete. If, as Constant says, we are made up of our contacts with others, then to break off with someone is to die a little, to give up this being which is the only one that we have. Life with Mme. de Malbée was painful, but it was his. To cut himself off from her definitively, to condemn her to fading memories, would be like cutting off a hand that had made him suffer. The part was not in the best shape, but it was there. Constant would write in his *Journal*, speaking of Mme. de Staël: " 'Minette' is part of me; I cannot rip her out of my existence" (June 1, 1805). Suffering, like joy, makes up our life; to deprive oneself of it is to cease living. The narrator thus clings, with all his strength, not to Mme. de Malbée but to his own past. He does not want to part with anything — which provokes the unhappiness of those who surround him. Once more, when holding onto the world of human finitude, the choice appears impossible, our principles do not allow us to decide. Therefore, we appeal to Heaven, but it remains silent.

The tale is interrupted in full anguish, in a desperate atmosphere: Cécile is between life and death, struck by what she has just understood (but we know that, unlike Ellénore, she will escape from the mess). This interruption obviously deprives us of the analysis that Constant would have provided of the shift of this sentiment. So rich in terms of questions raised, *Cécile* leaves us a little bit hungry.

Laughter and Tears

Ma Vie, which probably dates back to 1811-1812, is also an interrupted autobiographical account, but here we are not abandoned in the middle of a dramatic development. It covers the first twenty years of Constant's life (until his departure for Brunswick), and all the characters bear their true names. This testifies that Constant cherished the idea of publishing an autobiography. The story develops as follows: the first seventeen years are referred to briefly (they take up only seven pages), the next two years a little more extensively (seven more pages) and all the rest of the text (approximately forty four pages in paperback edition) is devoted to the twentieth year of the author's life. Once again we find the simplicity of style, the taste for precision, the keenness of observation.

What is new compared to *Cécile* is the alternation of the tone and the episodes. They are of two different types, some comic and picaresque, others tender and idyllic. It is here that Constant reveals his capacity for humor, for the first time. The narrator pokes fun at himself, above all. His first love affairs are situations in which we find him playing a ridiculous role: despairing suitor of "the commander's daughter," who nevertheless quickly finds comfort; companion of a girl with a "bad reputation" and "apparently the only man whom she resisted" (91); madly in love with Mme. Trevor, who would eagerly yield to him but from whom he recoils every time she tries to approach him; angling for money from Mme. Saurin who believes that he is coming to declare his love; pathetic and grotesque, finally, with Mlle. Pourrat and her mother, looking to take the daughter away without ever asking her opinion, attempting to commit suicide in front of the mother before going to the Opera with her! The ridiculous side of the character does not stop there: he is regularly robbed and hoodwinked, he accumulates empty promises and gambling debts, not to mention extravagant gestures like the ill-considered purchase of a monkey. . . It is true that the author's mockeries are not limited to himself; he also makes fun of his tutors and various other characters met along the way. Together, these episodes create an appealing, droll account, where the author's self-irony engages the reader's sympathy.

These entertaining adventures, which one has the impression may have been told many times in friendly company before being written down, alternate with others in a contrastingly tender emotion. Only one of them has to do with love. It is the meeting with Mme. Johannot, described in terms similar to those that had referred to Cécile. "She did not make me purchase the tender feelings she gave me with any mixture of agitation or sorrow" (94). For that matter, there was a similar moment of happiness in *Cécile,* when the two lovers went to a masked ball and enjoyed their secret intimacy in the middle of a crowd. "This way of existing only for one another, across the floods of the multitude, seemed to us a closer union, and filled our hearts with pleasure and love" (VI, 166). It is also the happiness that the narrator experiences, twice, in the midst of his friends in Edinburgh. And finally there is the peaceful voyage through the English countryside, mounted on a small white horse. "The whole way was delicious" (*Ma Vie,* 121). The alternation of the two types of episodes, comic and idyllic, prevents any monotony and renders this autobiographical account particularly endearing.

Some characters escape derision as well as idealization. Thus Mme. de Charrière, whom one finds here for the third time, now under her true name: a mocking and cynical spirit, filled with contempt for all prejudices and finally for mankind itself. Thus the narrator's father, present initially through the cascade of tutors, disparaged as soon as appointed, then in a strong scene where the son expects an explanation, whereas the father retains his cold politeness (his timidity obviously the model for that of Adolphe's father). Finally and especially, the narrator himself, although here Constant chooses the description of the facts rather than introspection. The narrator is a two-sided being, still more so than he was in *Cécile*, or in *Adolphe*. One thus finds an oscillation between the rejection of loneliness and the taste for independence, the strongest commitment alternating with sudden moments of doubt. Long periods of "idleness" are interrupted by sudden passions. The tender observer of the human comedy can state abruptly, as did the narrator of *Cécile*: "I treat myself lightly because I barely find myself interesting; I listen to others peacefully, because they do not interest me at all" (I, 140). The joy of living one's life hides "a secret desire to get out of it" (*Ma Vie*, 132). This duplicity, potentially dramatic, clashes with the vivacious tone of the picaresque tale.

The same change of tone is produced by the evocation of the later destiny of the characters. Already in *Adolphe*, the narrator depreciated the present experience by recalling the inevitability of death. "I revolt against life as if life were not going to end!" (VII, 60). In *Ma Vie*, an impressive number of characters end badly, long after the events depicted by the tale. M. Duplessis "ends up blowing his brains out" (89), John Wilde "becomes a raging madman," "chained in a dungeon on a pile of straw" (92), Mme. Johannot poisons herself, "believing herself to have been forgotten and abandoned by everyone on earth" (94), Mme. Trevor is "practically insane from fits of hysterics" (98). Thus behind this merry account of youthful adventures lurks a reminder that a generally not very amusing destiny awaits us: death, madness, suffering. "Poor wretch mankind, so much for us and our aspirations!" (92).

A certain surprise thus awaits us at the end of Constant's two autobiographical writings: the idyll devolves into a menace. *Cécile* was to be the account of happiness; it comes to a stop amid the oppression born of the impossibility of taking action. *Ma Vie* refers to the joys and the laughter of youth; but those who used to laugh suffer and cry today. Earthly life is the only one we have, and there are innumerable ways to spoil it. At the dawn of his literary career, in 1786, Constant said to his cousin Charles: "All men are unhappy, [. . .] all of human nature conspires for our misfortune" (Rudler, 143).

Morality and Truth

In conclusion, let us return to Constant's body of thought. If one considers the whole of his work, one realizes that morality need not be restricted only to compassion any more than it necessarily requires faith in immortality and the Divine. To assess it requires only that we think of the community of mankind, of which each one necessarily is a part and which at the same time forms a part of each one. Constant's doctrines are, in this respect, in line with the humanistic thought represented most visibly in France by Rousseau. This thought is stated, once more, in the face of two-fold opposition: one cannot understand mankind without taking account of his need for transcendence, of values that are to be found beyond egoistic concerns. However, this transcendence can be purely human, it does not have to be accompanied by religious faith. This path, equally distant from materialist nihilism and from religious dogmatism, is not a path strewn with roses. Men are imperfect, their feelings remain inconstant and uncertain, love more often ends in failure and resignation that in lasting happiness. Nevertheless, that is the path that embodies the vocation of modern man.

To Love Truth – Or Your Neighbor

What, then, is the place of morality in our life? Constant proposes to distinguish between two complementary, mutually exclusive perspectives on our universe. The first is that of the objective world; the second, that of the human-subject who lives there. The second is not simply a road leading toward the first, in the way that imperfect attempts may lead to success. It has, quite apart, its own ideal. The first perspective is that of science (Constant says philosophy) and its goal is truth. The second is that of morality (and thus, historically, of religion), which aspires not to truth but to goodness. The choice between the two depends on which goal we pursue.

Here, first, is their description, projected on the history of religions. Constant considers that Greek polytheism had become the face worn by their philosophical and scientific spirit; whereas Christianity embodied the moral requirement:

> In the old belief [polytheism,] that philosophy had subjugated, man was reduced to the rank of an imperceptible atom in the vastness of the universe. The new form

> [Christianity] puts him back at the center of a world that
> was created only for him: he is at the same time God's
> creation and God's goal. The philosophical concept is
> perhaps the truer; but the other one is so much fuller
> with warmth and life; and, from a certain point of view,
> it also represents a higher and more sublime truth. If
> we consider grandeur for what it really is, there is more
> grandeur in a proud thought, in a profound emotion, in
> an act of devotion, than in the whole mechanism of the
> celestial spheres *(Religion,* I, I, 5, 99-100).

Man is only an atom lost in the universe, it is true,
but the human world is not (simply) that of truth, it is
also that of warmth and grandeur. Morality and science do not have to be subjected one to the other, and if
one adheres to the strictly human perspective, morality
has a higher value. There cannot be any humanistic science (Constant is passionate about the knowledge of
mankind, but that has nothing to do with morality); humanistic morality, on the other hand, is that which
makes man "the center of the world," "God's goal."

Constant had already noted this distinction, in the
context of a political argument, in one of his very first
publications when he was barely thirty years old. He
insisted on the need to introduce what he called
"intermediate principles" between the abstract postu-
lates and the specific facts; and he illustrated this need
with a critique of one of Kant's theses:

> If the moral principle, that is, truth as a duty, for exam-
> ple, were taken as an absolute and in isolation, it would

> make any society impossible. We have the proof of that
> in the very direct consequences that a German philoso-
> pher derived from this principle, going so far as to claim
> that if assassins asked you whether your friend whom
> they are pursuing has taken refuge in your house, your
> lie would be a crime (*Réactions politiques*, VIII, 136).

The absurdity of such a consequence leads Constant to locate the general principle within a suitable
framework. Truth can be an obligation only within a
society, where individuals cooperate among themselves. Assassins and their victims do not form a society, they are rather like two countries at war; no moral
obligation holds anymore. "Thus, one can say that
truth is a duty only towards those who are entitled to
truth. However, no man is entitled to a truth that
harms others" (137). The principle of society overrides
that of truth, the requirement for friendship authorizes
the lie.

Having become aware of Constant's argument,
Kant felt stung, and replied in the same year of 1797 by
way of a minor work entitled *Sur un prétendu droit de
mentir par humanité*. What disturbed Kant above all was
Constant's use of everyday immediate experience; for
Kant, principles arise from reason, and have nothing to
do with the possible observation of individual suffering
(here, the death of the persecuted). Kant is not interested in the practical consequences of actions. To lie is,
in itself, contrary to the principles of the good life,
whatever the circumstances. The hierarchy of values

embraced by Constant is different: not to harm others is the aim — which can often be well served by veracity (for instance, in all contractual relations), at other times by lying (for instance, to assassins). The *you*, not the *I*, constitutes the ultimate proof of morality; other people's happiness carries more weight than my own perfection (to use the Kantian vocabulary). This is why love for your neighbor must prevail, according to Constant, over love for the truth. Anything, rather than to make others suffer: this can also make suicide virtuous. "He who feels that, at the prospect of torture, he would betray friendship, would denounce the unfortunate ones, would violate the secrets entrusted to his keeping, fulfills a duty by taking his own life" (*Religion*, V, XIII, 4, 75). All other principles yield before this one.

Relations between two individuals are not a matter for the objective perspective of science — they do not aspire to the truth but obey the requirements of friendship. From this point of view, the care which Constant takes to avoid irritating his close relations takes on more meaning. Other people's suffering should not dictate all of my behavior, for it may be real or pretended or both, may be endured or chosen or both, and may increase or decrease the suffering of a third party — who is also an *other*. We must qualify the general postulate by an "intermediate principle," as Constant would say. It is no less true that, in my behavior towards others, I let myself be guided by the principle of the good, not by that of truth. Julie Talma, Constant's best friend, is dying under his eyes. Must he tell her? "I wondered whether truth were not a duty; but what would have been the result of a truth that Julie was afraid of hearing?" (*Julie*, 198). Love, friendship, affection override duty. Germaine de Staël, with whom he lives, has interests incompatible with his. Must he dot every "i"? "I do not say anything that is not true, but I do not say the whole truth" (to Rosalie Constant, July 23, 1803). Perhaps he is mistaken in the choices that he makes, but he does not give up his principle. "You would say that there is duplicity in my behavior; but with a passionate person, duplicity that spares them sorrow appears me to be better than a frankness that would do more harm" (to the countess of Nassau, July 13, 1809). As regards passion, truth does not take priority. "I am the truest man in the world, except in love," Constant writes in his diary (April 13, 1805).

A Man of Dialogue

In the private world, the obligation to tell the truth plays only a subordinate role. In the public world, it is not telling the truth that is essential, but having the possibility to seek it. Like Lessing, Constant could proclaim: truth is appropriate only to the gods; it is the search for truth that is the properly human task. He devotes a section of his 1806 *Principes de politique* to this question. Persisting in an error, certainly, is disastrous for the public spirit. But imposing an already established truth is no less so. Truth concerns the objective world, not life in society; the benefit of its knowledge would be cancelled by its mode of social existence, the obligation inflicted by authority. The absence of truth is harmful but, if one engages in seeking the truth rather than merely submitting oneself to it, one also accepts what constitutes its "natural path": "reasoning, comparison, examination" (XIV, 3, 362). The effect of the method here bears upon its own result. Constant concludes, "Errors freely made are better than imposed truth" (*Filangieri*, IV, 6, 408). Controlled truth is sterile, while free exploration is fertile, and we have seen that, for Constant, the true virtue of freedom lies precisely in that it allows every opinion to be examined, every debate to be pursued. And here is the paradox: "If it were necessary to choose between persecution and protection, persecution would be better for our enlightenment" (*Principes*, 1806, XIV, 4, 368).

Constant does not say, "every one believes his own truth, and it is better that way." Rather: the free confrontation of opinions, the argued and contradictory debate, the critical dialogue respectful of the adversary constitute a social value higher than the accession to a truth dogmatically affirmed, whether it be a divine revelation or an axiom imposed by the State. "Truth is especially valuable because of the activity that is inspired in man by the need to discover it" *(Dunoyer,* 561). The debate, which is only the means, here becomes the end. If there is an ultimate antagonism between truth and humanity, Constant chooses humanity.

This is why Constant casts a critical eye on many contemporary philosophers. They claim to serve humanity by seeking truth, but their formulations are so dogmatic that they cancel out the intended effect:

> The new German philosophy [here, Constant is thinking
> of Fichte, Schelling, and the Schlegel brothers] has two
> or three great ideas, but its spirit of persecution is more
> dangerous than any of the truths (that the new German
> philosophy claims to discover) could ever be useful.
> For even the way in which it establishes the truth is the
> opposite of a calm quest conducted in good faith. The
> truth established by these gentlemen has all the disad-
> vantages of this error; and they have at the same time
> the arrogance of philosophers and the tricks of inquisi-
> tors (*Journal*, August 25, 1804).

This is also why Constant disapproves of the way
in which conversations in France are usually conducted.
Every one tries to be witty at the expense of the others,
rather than to maintain the human exchange itself,
guided by the search for truth and respect for others.

> Words of this kind, striking in themselves, have the dis-
> advantage of killing the conversation. They are, so to
> speak, rifle shots that one fires on other people's ideas,
> and which cut them down (*Julie*, 190-191).

Now, the humanity of the interlocutors is higher
than the beauty of the words and truth of the ideas.

But, with Constant, there is no need to separate the
search for truth from concern for humanity; besides,
that would be impossible. The life of the spirit is not
isolated from social existence by an impermeable barrier. Indeed, that is why Constant appears to us as a
man of dialogue, above all: impassioned no less by in-

teraction with others than by the search for truth. He seeks it through discussion — with Montesquieu and Rousseau, his great predecessors; with Germaine de Staël, accomplice and friend; with Goethe, whom he met in Weimar, and who remembers Constant precisely as a man of dialogue; with the contemporary authors whose works he translates and comments upon. To advance his own thought, he tirelessly confronts that of his peers, Bentham and Godwin, Filangieri and Schlegel, and even Bonald and Lamennais, and the Saint-Simonians.

From this manifold work emerges the face of an author who, today, far from remaining fixed on an inaccessible pedestal, seems singularly close to us, in his constant questioning as well as in his vulnerability. Did Constant attain that triple force that he wished to find among his contemporaries — fidelity in love, religious belief, the passion for freedom? One cannot answer in one word. The philosopher and the writer found ways to open new avenues that permitted democratic man to face, without too much fear, the challenges that await him: he knows that there is a form of politics that guarantees the dignity of the individual without dissolving the social bond, a religion that is stripped of its oppressive forms, a love that can give meaning to existence. Constant the individual, like each of us, succeeded more or less in conforming to his own ideal. He fought relentlessly, throughout his entire life, for freedom; nobody in France has contributed as much to its defense.

Faith, for him, is always mixed with doubt; as for his love affairs, they are fragile and cause suffering more often than serenity: the original wound is difficult to heal. What distinguishes him from other men is not the imperfection but the desire to live in his time and to understand it, the exceptional lucidity in regard to himself and the courage with which he decides to reveal himself, and the eloquence that results. Constant was by no means a saint, nor even a sage; he is, however, a man who allows us to understand our destiny better and to accept it.

And if we had to hold onto only one sentence as an emblem of his destiny, I would keep this one, which he addressed one day to his friend Annette de Gérando (June 5, 1815):

> I always found a word, a glance, a handshake preferable to all of reason and to all the thrones on earth.

Chronology

1767

October 25. Benjamin is born in Lausanne, to Henriette-Pauline de Chandieu and Juste Constant de Rebecque, career soldier. His parents are Protestants of French extraction.

November 10. His mother dies. Benjamin is raised by his grandmothers.

1772

The father entrusts the education of his son to his mistress, Marianne Magnin (with whom he will have two more children), and to various tutors.

1774-1781

Stays in the Netherlands (where his father is garrisoned), in Brussels, in England and Switzerland, according to his father's will. In 1779, he composes his first work, *Les Chevaliers*, a heroic novel in verse.

1782

Enrolls at the University of Erlangen.

1783

Arrives in July at Edinburgh, where he stays at the university for nearly two years. He participates in many activities and makes strong friendships.

1785

May-August. Stays in Paris, establishes acquaintances in the literary and philosophical milieux.

August. Sets out again for Brussels, where he has a liaison with Mme. Johannot, then returns to the Netherlands and to Switzerland.

November. Starts work on a piece on polytheism which, in various forms, will occupy him throughout his entire life.

1786

Stays in Switzerland (where he meets Mme. Trevor), then, at the end of the year, heads for Paris.

1787

Joins the Parisian literary circles, where he becomes acquainted with Isabelle de Charrière, a woman of letters, 27 years his elder, who makes quite an impression.

May-June. Tries in vain to court Mlle. Pourrat.

June. A summons from his father impels him to leave for England by himself, where he remains for three months (this is the voyage described in *Ma Vie* and in the letters to Isabelle de Charrière).

September. Rejoins his father, stays in Switzerland.

1788

February. His father installs him at the court of the duke of Brunswick, where he receives the title of chamberlain. He will remain there, intermittently, until 1794.

November. Becomes engaged to Minna von Cramm, whom he will marry the following year.

1789
First estrangements with Isabelle de Charrière. He actively intercedes in his father's lawsuits, pursued by his military superiors. Follows with interest the events in France.

1790-1792
Prepares a refutation of Burke's book on the French revolution, which he will never complete. His marital life deteriorates.

1793
Meets Charlotte von Hardenberg, his future second wife; separates from Minna. The life of politics interests him more and more. He remains in Switzerland a long time.

1794
Works on his book on religion.

September. Meets Germaine de Staël, daughter of the minister Necker, wife of the ambassador of Sweden in Paris, and already author of several notable works. He immediately falls in love with her. He is delighted by the end of the Terror in France.

1795
Settles in with Germaine de Staël, without being her lover.

May. He follows her to Paris, where he stays until December. He keeps company with the former Girondins, including Jean Baptiste Louvet, President of the Convention. First political publications.

1796
Back in Switzerland, he publishes his first pamphlet, *De la force du gouvernement actuel . . .*

April. Becomes Germaine de Staël's lover, with whom he is also engaged in active intellectual collaboration. Several trips between Paris and Switzerland.

1797
Settled in France, he publishes a new pamphlet, *Des réactions politiques*. Kant, indirectly challenged, replies at once. Constant stands as a candidate in various elections, and is deeply engaged in political activity.

June. Birth of Albertine, daughter of Germaine and Benjamin.

1798
Intense political activities. Cooling of relations with Germaine. Meets Julie Talma, who will become one of his most faithful friends. Publish a new pamphlet, *Des suites de la contre-révolution de 1660 en Angleterre*. Begins the translation of *Political Justice* by S. Godwin.

1799
Stays sometimes in France, sometimes in Switzerland, often with Germaine de Staël. Finishes translating Godwin, engages in writing his first great political treatise, dedicated to the republican constitution.

November. Coup d'état of the 18th Brumaire, Bonaparte takes power. In December, Constant is appointed to the Tribunat, an advisory institution.

1800
Many speeches to the Tribunat. Works on his political treatise.

November. Beginning of the affair with Anna Lindsay, which will continue until the following summer.

1801
Speeches to the Tribunat. He comes closer to the Ideologists

group.

1802

January. Eliminated from the Tribunat by Bonaparte, at the same time as other opposing members.

Stays in Switzerland, where he probably finishes his work on the republican constitution.

1803

Dreams of marrying Amélie Fabbri to escape from Germaine, hesitations consigned in the journal entitled *Amélie et Germaine.* Mme. De Staël is prohibited from staying in Paris.

October. Germaine and Benjamin leave for Germany. They go to Weimar and to Jena, where they become acquainted with Goethe, Schiller, the Schlegel brothers, Schelling and Wieland.

1804

Still in Germany, works on the book on religion.

May. Returns to Switzerland, visits France.

1805

Takes up with Charlotte again, whom he plans to marry. Death of Julie Talma and Isabelle de Charrière (from whom he had distanced himself since 1794).

1806

February-August. Writes *Principes de politique,* his great treatise on political philosophy.

November-December. Fiction writing, which eventually results in *Adolphe* and *Cécile.*

1807

Intense relations with Charlotte, interminable arguments with Germaine. Various literary labors including an amendment of Schiller's *Wallenstein*, under the title of *Wallstein*.

September-October. Pietist episode in Switzerland.

1808
June. Secret marriage with Charlotte.

1809-1810
Vascillates between Charlotte and Germaine. Works on the book devoted to religion.

1811
May. Final separation from Germaine de Staël, departure with Charlotte in Germany. They settle in Göttingen. He continues working on the work on religion and probably writes *Ma Vie*.

1812
Death of his father, with whom the relations were always difficult. Continuation of the work on religion.

1813
Writes *Le Siège de Soissons,* an epic and satirical poem, then returns to his work on religion.

November. Meets Bernadotte, royal prince of Sweden, who he hopes will succeed Bonaparte.

November-December. Writes *De l'esprit de conquête et de l'usurpation,* an anti-Napoleonic work, actually made up for most part of extracts from the unpublished treatise *Principes de Politique.* It is published in April of the following year.

1814
Arriving in Paris in April, he seeks to play a part in politics. Publishes several texts on the freedom of the press.

September. Falls head over heels in love with Juliette Récamier, friend of Germaine de Staël, whom he has known for a long time.

1815

Publishes *De la responsabilité des ministres,* works on *Mémoires de Juliette.*

March. Bonaparte arrives in France, Constant publishes two anti-Napoleonic articles.

April. Agrees to become a State councillor and works on the *Acte additionnel* to the Constitution.

May. Publishes the *Principes de politique,* extracts of the great work of 1806, still in an anti-Napoleonic spirit.

July. After Bonaparte's abdication, writes an *Apologie,* presented to the king who has returned to France.

September. A new pietist episode, related to Mme. de Krüdener.

November. Finally manages to tear himself away from Paris and his unhappy love for Juliette. He leaves for Brussels where he meets up with Charlotte.

1816

January. The couple goes to London.

June. Adolphe appears in London and in Paris. Constant is at work on the *Lettres sur les Cent-Jours.*

September. The couple returns to Paris. Constant stops keeping his *Journal intime.*

1817

Intense journalistic activities, in *Mercure de France.*

July. Death of Germaine de Staël, on whom he publishes two long articles.

He becomes one of the leaders of the liberal party.

1818

Gathers his political publications under the title *Cours de politique constitutionnelle* (four volumes). Brings out a new periodical, *Minerve*. Many articles and pamphlets. Tries without success to be elected as a deputy.

June. An accident disables him; henceforth he requires crutches.

1819
February. Gives his lecture,*La Liberté des Anciens et des Modernes.*

March. Elected a deputy. Many speeches in the Chamber. Actively engages in the campaign against the slave trade.

1820-1821
Non-stop political activities, speeches in the Chamber of Deputies, publications in the press.

1822
Begins to publish his *Commentaire sur l'ouvrage de Filangieri,* where he once again systematically expounds his political theories.

November. Constant fails in the elections.

1823
He returns to his work on religion and decides its final plan. The five volumes which he prepares for printing will come out starting in the next year.

1824
Re-elected Deputy. Again, many speeches in the Chamber, although his health is deteriorating more and more.

1825-1829
Divides his time between preparing to publish the manuscript on religion, writing speeches and political articles, and looking after his health.

1830
Following the July Revolution, he supports the new king

Louis-Philippe. The latter grants him an allowance, enabling him to pay off the gambling debts that he has racked up over the course of his lifetime.

December 8. Dies in Paris. His funeral stirs the hearts of the nation.

Constant's Works

References and abbreviations

In the absence of any standard edition of Constant's writings, one is obliged to consult very diverse publications, some of them long unobtainable. Unless otherwise specified, the place of publication is Paris. When necessary, I indicate the abbreviation used in this book for each work.

I. Collections

Ecrits et discours politiques, J. J. Pauvert, 1964, 2 vol. (contains a useful selection of Benjamin Constant's speeches of 1800-1801 and 1824-1830).

Force = *De la force du gouvernement actuel de la France,* etc., Flammarion-Champs, 1988.

Modernes = *De la liberté chez les Modernes,* LGF-Livre de Poche-Pluriel, 1980 (republished in 1997 by Gallimard-Folio under the title *Ecrits politiques*).

OC = *Œuvres complètes,* Tübingen, M. Niemeyer, 1993 s.

Œuvres = *Œuvres,* Gallimard-Pléiade, 1979. (*Adolphe*, *Cécile* and *Ma Vie* are also available in a volume in the "Folio" collection.)

Portraits = *Portraits. Mémoires. Souvenirs,* Champion, 1992.

Recueil = *Recueil d'articles 1795-1817,* Geneva, Droz, 1978 (six other collections of articles were published, all under the direction of E. Harpaz, all at Droz, between 1972 and 1992).

II. Individual Publications

A. Works

Conquête = *De l'esprit de conquête et de l'usurpation,* Garnier-Flammarion, 1986.

Constitution républicaine = *Fragments d'un ouvrage abandonné sur la possibilité d'une constitution républicaine dans un grand pays,* Aubier, 1991.

Filangieri = G. Filangieri, *Œuvres,* Vol. III, 1840, commentary by Benjamin Constant.

Polythéisme = *Du polythéisme romain,* 2 vols., 1833.

Principes 1806 = *Principes de politique applicables à tous les gouvernements,* Genève, Droz, 1980; republished in 1997 by Hachette-Pluriel.

Religion = *De la religion considérée dans sa source, ses formes et ses développements,* Vol. I, 1824; Vol. II, 1825; Vol. III, 1827, Vols. IV and V, 1831.

B. Correspondence

"Lettres à Prosper de Barante," *Revue des Deux Mondes,* July 15 and August 1, 1906.

"Letters to Isabelle de Charrière," in: I. de Charrière, *Œuvres complètes.* Amsterdam, G. A. Van Oorschot and Geneva, Slatkine, in particular Vol. III, 1981 and Vol. IV, 1982.

Benjamin and Rosalie de Constant, *Correspondance.* Gallimard, 1955.

Journal intime de Benjamin Constant et lettres à sa famille et à ses amis, 1895.

Lettres de Benjamin Constant à sa famille, 1775-1830, Stock, 1931 (these two publications are quite flawed; however, they contain the letters to his aunt, the countess of Nassau, which are of interest).

Benjamin Constant and Mme. Récamier, *Lettres 1807-1830,* Champion, 1992 (also contains his letters to Annette de Gérando).

Benjamin Constant and Mme. de Staël, *Lettres à un ami (Claude Hochet),* Neuchâtel, à la Baconnière, 1949.

III. Specific Texts

Adolphe, in*: Œuvres.*

Amélie et Germaine, in: *Œuvres.*

Article = article in the *Journal des débats,* March 19, 1815, in: *Recueil.*

Cécile, in: *Œuvres.*

Cent-Jours = *Mémoires sur les Cent-Jours: OC,* Vol. XIV, 1993.

Dunoyer = *De M. Dunoyer et de quelques-uns de ses ouvrages,* in: *Modernes.*

Education = *De la juridiction du gouvernement sur l'éducation,* in: *Modernes.*

Godwin = *De Godwin et de son ouvrage sur la justice politique,* in: *Modernes.*

Guerre de Trente Ans, in: *Œuvres*

Histoire abrégée de l'égalité, in : *OC,* Vol. III, 1995.

Idées religieuses = *Du développement progressif des idées religieuses,* in: *Modernes*

Journal, in: *Œuvres*.

Julie = *Lettre sur Julie*, in: *Portraits*.

Liberté = *De la liberté des Anciens comparée à celle des Modernes*, in: *Modernes*.

Liberté politique = *La Liberté politique, essentielle à la liberté civile*, in: *Recueil*.

Littérature du XVIII siècle = *Esquisse d'un essai sur la littérature du XVIII siècle*, in: *OC*, Vol. III, vol. I, 1995.

Ma Vie, in: *Œuvres* (under the title *Le Cahier rouge*).

Mémoires de Juliette, in: *Portraits*.

Madame de Staël = *De madame de Staël et de ses ouvrages*, in: *Portraits*.

Passions religieuses = *Des passions religieuses et de leurs rapports avec la morale*, in: *P. Déguise, Benjamin Constant inconnu*, Geneva, Droz, 1966.

Pensées détachées, in: *Modernes*.

Perfectibility I = *De la perfectibilité de l'espèce humaine*, in: *Modernes*.

Perfectibility II = *Fragment d'un essai sur la perfectibilité de l'espèce humaine*, in: *Modernes*.

Préface abandonnée d'Adolphe in: *OC*, Vol. III, t. 1, 1995.

Préface aux Mélanges, in: *Modernes*.

Principes = *Principes de politique*, in: *Modernes*.

Souvenirs historiques, in: *Portraits*.

Sur la censure des journaux, in: *Œuvres*.

Tragédie = *Réflexions sur la tragédie*, in: *Œuvres*

J. Wilde, in: *OC, série Correspondance générale*, Vol. I, 1993.

IV. A Selection of Constant's Works in English Trans-

lation

Adolphe. New York: B. Blackwell, 1989.

Adolphe and *The Red Notebook* (= *Ma Vie*) With an introduction by Harold Nicolson. New York: New American Library, 1959; and Indianapolis: Bobbs-Merrill, 1959.

Cecile. Edited and annotated by Alfred Roulin; translated by Norman Cameron. Norfolk, CT: James Laughlin, 1953

Political Writings. New York: Cambridge University Press, 1988

Prophecy from the Past: Benjamin Constant on conquest and usurpation, edited and translated by Helen Byrne Lippmann. New York: Reynal & Hitchcock, c. 1941.

V. Other Authors Cited

Condorcet, "Mémoires sur l'instruction publique," *Œuvres complètes,* Vol. VII, 1849.

I. Kant, "Sur un prétendu droit de mentir par droit de mentir par humanité," *Œuvres complètes,* Gallimard-Pléiade, Vol. III, 1986. In English see: "On a supposed right to lie because of philanthropic concerns" in *Grounding for the metaphysics of morals,* translated by James W. Ellington, Indianapolis: Hackett Pub. Co., c. 1993.

J. J. Rousseau, *Œuvres complètes,* Gallimard-Pléiade, Vol. II, 1964 *(La Nouvelle Héloïse),* Vol. III, 1964 *(Discours sur l'origine de l'inégalité, Le Contrat Social),* Vol. IV, 1969 *(Emile).*

Stendhal, *Courrier anglais,* Vol. V, Le Divan, 1936.

Selective Bibliography

Reference works:

- C. COURTNEY, *A Bibliography of Editions of the Writings of Benjamin Constant to 1833.* London: The Modern Humanities Research Association, 1981.
- E. HOFMANN *(under the direction of), Bibliographie analytique des écrits sur Benjamin Constant, 1796-1980.* Lausanne: Institut Benjamin-Constant, and Oxford: The Voltaire Foundation, 1980.

A more succinct bibliography may be found in the above-mentioned edition of *L'Esprit de conquête,* p. 301-319, by Ephraïm Harpaz.

- D. VERREY, *Chronologie de la vie et de l'oeuvre de Benjamin Constant,* Vol. I, 1767-1805. Geneva: Slatkine, 1992.

Annales Benjamin Constant, a magazine dedicated to studies of Constant (published in Lausanne since 1980).

The notes and forewords accompanying recent republications of Constant's works are also helpful in determining how to approach his thought.

Two general studies have the merit of taking into account the various facets of his work:

- G. POULET, *Benjamin Constant par lui-même*. Le Seuil, 1968.
- B. FONTANA, *Benjamin Constant and the Post-Revolutionary Mind*, New Haven and London: Yale University Press, 1991.

Two recent biographies are conveniently complementary, one focusing on his doctrines, the other on his life.

- K. KLOOKE, *Benjamin Constant, Une biographie intellectuelle*, Geneva: Droz, 1984.
- D. Wood, *Benjamin Constant, A Biography*, London & New York: Routledge, 1993.

On the first years of his life, the best reference work is:

- G. RUDLER, *La Jeunesse de Benjamin Constant*. A. Colin, 1908.

On the beginnings of his political life and love life, an excellent clarification:

- B.W. JASINSKI, *L'Engagement de Benjamin Constant*. Minard, 1971.

On the role of the mother in Constant's work:

- H. VERHOEFF, *"Adolphe" et Constant: une étude psychocritique*. Klincksieck, 1976.

On political thought, see in particular:

- S. HOLMES, *Benjamin Constant and the Making of Modern Liberalism*. New Haven: Yale University Press, 1984. The studies by M. Gauchet, Ph. Reynaud, and P. Manent contributed to awakening interest in France for Constant's political thought.

On the history of political and social thought at the time of Constant, the standard work is:

- P. BÉNICHOU, *Le Temps des prophètes.* Gallimard, 1977.

On Constant's writings devoted to religion, two works also complementary, one more historical, the other more systematic:

- P. DÉGUISE, *Benjamin Constant méconnu.* Genève: Droz, 1966.
- H. GOUHIER, *Benjamin Constant.* Desclée de Brouwer (Les écrivains devant Dieu), 1967.

On the *Journal intime* and its place among other diaries of the time:

- A. GIRARD, *Le Journal intime.* PUF, 1963.

On *Adolphe,* see the voluminous study:

- P. DELBOUILLE, *Genèse, structure et destin d' "Adolphe."* Les Belles Lettres, 1971

Other books from Algora Publishing

CLAUDIU A. SECARA
THE NEW COMMONWEALTH

From Bureaucratic Corporatism to Socialist Capitalism

The notion of an elite-driven worldwide perestroika has gained some credibility lately. The book examines in a historical perspective the most intriguing dialectic in the Soviet Union's "collapse" — from socialism to capitalism and back to socialist capitalism — and speculates on the global implications.

IGNACIO RAMONET
THE GEOPOLITICS OF CHAOS

The author, Director of *Le Monde Diplomatique,* presents an original, discriminating and lucid political matrix for understanding what he calls the "current disorder of the world" in terms of Internationalization, Cyberculture and Political Chaos.

MICHEL PINÇON & MONIQUE PINÇON-CHARLOT
GRAND FORTUNES

Dynasties of Wealth in France

Going back for generations, the fortunes of great families consist of far more than money—they are also symbols of culture and social interaction. They are at the heart of dense family and extra-family networks, of international coalitions and divisions. The authors elucidate the machinery of accumulation and the paradoxically quasi-collective nature of private fortunes.

CLAUDIU A. SECARA
TIME & EGO
Judeo-Christian Egotheism and the Anglo-Saxon Industrial Revolution

The first question of abstract reflection that arouses controversy is the problem of Becoming. Being persists, beings constantly change; they are born and they pass away. How can Being change and yet be eternal? The quest for the logical and experimental answer has just taken off.

JEAN-JACQUES ROSA
EURO ERROR

Is there still a choice? The Euro is being adopted by governments, the media, and even by European citizens. They promise us less unemployment and more freedom. But are we so certain of the outcome?

JEAN-MARIE ABGRALL
SOUL SNATCHERS: THE MECHANICS OF CULTS

Jean-Marie Abgrall, psychiatrist, criminologist, expert witness to the French Court of Appeals, and member of the Inter-Ministry Committee on Cults, is one of the experts most frequently consulted by the European judicial and legislative processes. The fruit of fifteen years of research, his book delivers the first methodical analysis of the sectarian phenomenon, decoding the mental manipulation on behalf of mystified observers as well as victims.

JEAN-CLAUDE GUILLEBAUD
THE TYRANNY OF PLEASURE

The ambition of the book is to pose clearly and without subterfuge the question of sexual morals -- that is, the place of the forbidden -- in a modern society. For almost a whole generation, we have lived in the illusion that this question had ceased to exist. Today the illusion is faded, but a strange and tumultuous distress replaces it. No longer knowing very clearly where we stand, our societies painfully seek answers between unacceptable alternatives: bold-faced permissiveness or nostalgic moralism.

SOPHIE COIGNARD & MARIE-THÉRÈSE GUICHARD
FRENCH CONNECTIONS

Networks of Influence

They were born in the same region, went to the same schools, fought the same fights and made the same mistakes in youth. They share the same morals, the same fantasies of success and the same taste for money. They act behind the scenes to help each other, boosting careers, monopolizing business and information, making money, conspiring and, why not, becoming Presidents!

VLADIMIR PLOUGIN
INTELLIGENCE HAS ALWAYS EXISTED

Mysterious episodes from Russia's past, from abductions and betrayals in Kievan Rus to Ivan the Terrible's secret service — intelligence and counterintelligence have been with us for a long time. Here, a Moscow State University historian presents some of the most tantalizing tales, based on original documents.